RECEPTION

RECEPTION

An Ecumenical Opportunity

WILLIAM G. RUSCH

THE LUTHERAN WORLD FEDERATION

Published by Fortress Press, Philadelphia, in cooperation with the Lutheran World Federation, 150 route de Ferney, 1211 Geneva 20, Switzerland.

LWF Report 22, 1988
ISSN 0174–1764

ISBN (Fortress Press)   0–8006–2091–7

Parallel edition in German:

Rezeption: Eine ökumenische Chance
LWB-Report 22, Stuttgart, 1988
ISSN 0172–5068

Printed in the United States of America

To Thora

CONTENTS

PREFACE

Reception, as both a word and a concept, is becoming increasingly important in ecumenical theology. After years of neglect, both the classical and ecumenical meanings of reception are again being explored. The past two decades have seen a marked increase in the literature devoted to reception. Most of this material is in specialized theological journals, and much of it is in German. In time a major work must be written that will examine in depth the history and ecumenical potential of reception. But it is probably still too early in the practice of ecumenical reception to expect such a volume today.

This modest-sized book seeks to review the discussions of reception in the periodical literature and to offer a number of suggestions for the future. I think of this volume as standing between the constantly growing body of articles about reception and the major treatise to be written eventually. My hope is that this work will not only offer a summary of the discussion to date but prompt churches and individuals to think carefully about reception and to begin to put it into practice.

For the preparation of this manuscript, I am once again grateful to Katherine Rabenau. She has been of invaluable asssistance as the material moved from written text to printed page. The Institute for Ecumenical Research at Strasbourg, and especially its director, Professor Harding Meyer, deserve a special word of thanks. I have always been welcomed at the Institute, and its library has been placed at my disposition.

INTRODUCTION

The subject of this book is a word and concept of ever-increasing interest in ecumenical circles: reception. In 1983 Thomas Ryan called "reception" the new "holy word" of the ecumenical movement.[1] Yet only some six years earlier Franz Wolfinger had wondered whether reception was forgotten in the church.[2] Obviously something was happening between 1977 and 1983, and the process has continued to accelerate.

To gain some perspective on what is meant by reception as it is discussed at present in ecumenical theology, this volume will concentrate on three areas: (1) the immediate context for the contemporary discussion of reception and the ideas associated with the word, (2) the earlier history of the word and concept, and (3) suggestions about the future of this word and concept in the ecumenical movement.

It is not surprising that something new is occurring on the ecumenical scene. As its very name implies, the ecumenical movement is not static. It is a living, growing process of bringing the churches that take part in it closer to visible unity. Since the beginnings of the modern ecumenical movement in 1910 it is possible to observe certain emphases and shifts. Such changes are perfectly natural. The initial preoccupation and indeed catalyst of the ecumenical movement was mission. The churches became interested in the ecumenical movement because the scandal of disunity hampered missionary efforts, and for

---

1. Thomas Ryan, "Reception: Unpacking the New Holy Word," *Ecumenism* 82 (1983): 27–34.

2. Franz Wolfinger, "Die Rezeption theologischer Einsichten und ihre theologische und ökumenische Bedeutung: Von der Einsicht zur Verwirklichung," *Catholica* 31 (1977): 202–33.

many years this is what motivated ecumenism. But even in the early years, other emphases were appearing. The issues of Faith and Order and of Life and Work soon found their appropriate places in the ecumenical movement. Emphases on mission and witness in the rapidly changing world of the 1960s were supplemented by ecclesiological issues as the Orthodox and Roman Catholic churches in different ways entered the ecumenical movement. The decade of the 1960s saw the formation and proliferation of theological dialogues, technical and official conversations between churches or confessions. During the 1960s and 1970s the Commission on Faith and Order of the World Council of Churches continued its work to call the churches to visible unity by endeavoring to resolve church-dividing issues involving faith and the ordering of the church. By the early 1980s the churches found themselves confronted by shelves of theological documentation that by and large called upon and challenged them to take some specific steps to remove the divisiveness of the past and to express their unity more fully. The contents of these documents had to be responded to and ultimately received or incorporated into the life of the churches on all levels in order to be truly meaningful. Thus, reception did not enter the present ecumenical scene as an abstract concept for reflection, away from the faith and life of the church. Reception became a preoccupation as the churches struggled to react appropriately to the work of bilateral dialogues and the document *Baptism, Eucharist and Ministry* from the Commission on Faith and Order of the World Council of Churches. But for all our preoccupation with it, the term "reception" remains difficult to define and is open to several interpretations. It is probably too early in the contemporary discussion to arrive at a final definition, but when one is reached, it will certainly include the notions both of the churches' receiving the results of the ecumenical movement and of the churches' being changed by those results.

Because the emergence of reception as a significant ecumenical challenge is so recent, this book makes no claim to be the final word on the subject; rather it seeks to be a contribution to the significant discussion now taking place. Its purpose is to provide clarification of the issues surrounding reception, an explanation of the concept's history, and some guidance for the future. To begin, it is necessary to explore the context of the present interest in reception.

1

THE PRESENT DISCUSSION

The history of the ecumenical movement has been told often. Although it is not necessary to repeat it here, it will be helpful to review some of its main events as we seek to understand the present ecumenical situation and the current interest in reception.

There have been some attempts to heal the splits that took place between the Eastern and Western churches from the eleventh through the thirteenth centuries, and the division of the Western church at the time of the sixteenth-century Reformation, but such efforts have usually been isolated and largely the work of committed individuals. Only in the twentieth century have the divided churches entered into the movement to unite Christians in a regular and continuing way.

The modern ecumenical movement came into being with the World Missionary Conference that met in Edinburgh in 1910. The next few decades experienced a flurry of ecumenical activities, including the encyclical of the church of Constantinople in 1920, an invitation to all the churches to form a league of churches; a World Conference on Life and Work in Stockholm in 1925; and two years later, the first World Conference on Faith and Order at Lausanne. By 1933, plans were being laid for a World Council of Churches. These efforts continued before and through World War II, and in 1948 the World Council came into being, uniting the work of Life and Work and Faith and Order. Thirteen years later the International Missionary Council was integrated into the World Council. After the first assembly of the council in Amsterdam in 1948, assemblies met at intervals of approximately seven years. By 1968 and the fourth assembly, in Uppsala, the World Council and much of the ecumenical movement were preoccupied with the important issues of a rapidly changing world. Considerable emphasis was placed upon world economic and social development, on the condemnation of racism, and on responsibility for the development of the Third World. Some individuals wondered during those years whether theological concerns for the unity of the church were not being neglected as other critical issues were addressed.

But events were occurring in the 1960s that brought with them a renewed interest in the theological aspects of the ecumenical movement. At the third assembly of the World Council of Churches, in New Delhi in 1961, four Orthodox churches—the churches of Romania, Poland, Bulgaria, and the patriarchate of Moscow—joined the council. Their presence, along with the patriarchate of Constantinople (a founding member of the council), helped to ensure that a balance would be struck between the equally important theological and social concerns in the work of the World Council. The sixties also saw the entry of the Roman Catholic church into the ecumenical movement. With Pope John XXIII's creation in 1960 of the Secretariat for Promoting Christian Unity, regular contact began between the Roman Catholic church and other churches. This was illustrated most visibly during the Second Vatican Council.

In fact it is in the calling of this council in January 1959 by Pope John XXIII that we find the first motivation for the contemporary attraction to reception. Prior to this time, reception was of little interest in theological circles. We have already noted the lament of Franz Wolfinger that reception was forgotten in the church.[1] His estimate, based on standard pre-1960 theological references, both Catholic and Protestant, is certainly correct. Apart from the reflections of some patristic and medieval scholars interested in church councils, discussion of reception was almost completely absent from the theological writing of the time. But the dramatic calling of the Second Vatican Council raised serious questions—not just for the Roman Catholic church but for the ecumenical movement—about the conciliar nature of the church, the teaching authority of the church, and how conciliar and other teachings were received into and made part of the life of the church. How did the early church receive the decisions of the great ecumenical councils? Could the answer to this question make a contribution to the divided churches seeking greater unity? Thus the concept of reception returned to the modern theological agenda closely

---

1. See p. 11 above.

linked with conciliarity, with the idea of Christians gathering under the guidance of the Holy Spirit for prayer, counsel, and decision.

The effects of the Second Vatican Council on theological thought and discussion were immediate and are easy to document. Even before the council began to meet in 1962, its impact was apparent in the appearance of a number of works that directly or indirectly raised the topic of reception. One of the first of these volumes, *Die ökumenischen Konzile*, edited by Hans J. Margull, appeared first in Europe in 1961 and was followed five years later by an American edition.[2] The book is a collection of essays on the nature and authority of church councils, by recognized scholars from the Anglican, Lutheran, Old Catholic, Orthodox, Reformed, and Roman Catholic churches. Prefaces to both the American and German editions made clear that the book was a direct response to questions raised by the calling of the Second Vatican Council and by the lack of ecumenical discussion about ecumenical councils.[3] While it is true that no essay in the volume deals exclusively with reception, the subject is touched upon repeatedly. Georg Kretschmar in his discussion of the councils of the ancient church notes, without further elaboration, the need for Spirit-wrought *reception* of conciliar decisions.[4] Later in the same chapter Kretschmar points out that reception is a constantly new task for all Christians, having as its norm the apostolic word. Decisions about which of the ancient councils were orthodox must constantly be made on the basis of whether or not they reproduced the apostolic word.[5] Edmund Schlink observes that reception has undergone many transformations in history. The concept of the reception of conciliar resolutions into imperial law did not correspond to the actual process of reception in the church. Conciliar history of the early church recognized that a council can err and that the reception of its resolutions by the churches, and by the people of the churches, is important. Schlink sees a parallel between the early church's understanding of reception and the need for resolutions of assemblies of the World

2. Hans J. Margull, ed., *Die ökumenischen Konzile* (Stuttgart: Evangelisches Verlagswerk, 1961). American ed.: *The Councils of the Church* (Philadelphia: Fortress Press, 1966).

3. Margull, ed., *Councils of the Church,* v, ix.

4. Ibid., 23.

5. Ibid., 80–81.

Council to be received by the member churches and not just by representatives at an assembly.[6] He also voices regret over the declaration of papal infallibility by the Roman Catholic church in the last century, because it set aside, in his opinion, the process of reception of conciliar decisions as practiced by the early church.[7] Although the essay by Emilianos, then bishop of Meloa, on councils in the Orthodox church does not specifically mention the word "reception," the concept receives attention.[8] Emilianos stresses the role in Orthodox thought of the Spirit in reception and the important place of both the bishops and the laity in the reception of the ecumenical councils of the Orthodox. The discussion in the book edited by Margull makes it clear that reception was becoming a topic on the agenda of ecumenical conversation. Although reception does not receive major treatment in its own right, and is closely linked with the role of councils in church history and in the ecumenical movement, something of its importance and some of its essential features are identified.

In the same year that *Die ökumenischen Konzile* was published, the assembly of the World Council of Churches met in New Delhi. Here again the influence of the recently summoned (but not yet meeting) Second Vatican Council was felt. The assembly requested that a study of synods and councils of the ancient church be undertaken. This was done because the World Council saw the life of contemporary churches to be shaped by the great decisions of the early centuries and because the assembly believed that historical consideration of the early period, accompanied by theological reflection, might uncover the roots of problems dividing the modern churches. The Commission on Faith and Order undertook this work at meetings in 1963 and 1964. A special group met in 1965 and 1966. The final report was approved by the commission in 1967 and published one year later under the title *Councils and the Ecumenical Movement*. There was included a series of lectures given during the meetings of the special group.[9]

The commission's final report, 'The Importance of the Conciliar Process in the Ancient Church for the Ecumenical Movement," con-

6. Ibid.

7. Ibid., 489.

8. Ibid., 338–69.

9. *Councils and the Ecumenical Movement,* World Council of Churches Studies 5 (Geneva: World Council of Churches, 1968).

centrates, as its title indicates, on conciliarity (the fact that the church in all times needs assemblies to represent it) and the relationship of councils to the unity of the church. It examines the patterns of councils and then turns to their authority and impact, taking up the question of reception.[10] This report defines reception as the process by which local churches accept the decision of a council and thereby recognize its authority. It is viewed not as something added to the inner authority of a council but as something that confirms it. A multiplex process not always occurring in the same way, reception has as its norm the ancient apostolic tradition. At its core it is a spiritual process. Its proof is precisely the long process of critical appropriation that both precedes formal reception and follows it.

Reception as a spiritual event corresponds to a council's claim to be the voice of the Holy Spirit. Reception is still an open process. Churches in the ecumenical movement find themselves in a process of continuing or renewed reception in which confessional divisions can be overcome as the process of critical mutual reception of old and newer councils takes place. The final report concludes with some comments on how conciliarity as a concept can aid the churches to move toward a true ecumenical council in the future.

One essay in the volume, "Reception: Prolegomena to a Systematic Study," by Werner Küppers, directly addresses reception.[11] Not surprisingly, the entire discussion is placed in the context of councils. Küppers examines reception as a theological problem concerning how a particular council, and ultimately a whole connected series of councils, acquired or failed to acquire the recognition and authority they might have expected on the basis of the early church's understanding of councils. Problems of vocabulary are indicated. Then an examination is made of the process of reception in the early church. A line of development is traced from the reception of the conciliar process by the various local synods, to the great ecumenical synods with the deep involvement of the emperor. Küppers sees the considerable importance of the postconciliar reception process for the consensus on the fundamental Trinitarian and christological questions, a consensus on which the unity of the church rests. Finally, Küppers turns to recep-

10. Ibid., 15–17.
11. Ibid., 76–98.

tion as it relates to church division and the new *oikumene*. He recognizes the need to make room for a new reception process in the new conciliar life of the churches. The new *oikumene* can only be the fruit of a new conciliar life and of a new reception process. Reception of the self-attesting truth of God and reception of church statements deriving from the *synodos*, that is, from the "coming together about this," belong indissolubly together. He concludes that the acknowledgment of this fact and compliance with it constitute one of the decisive tasks in the struggle for Christian unity.[12] Thus the earliest attention to reception by the World Council of Churches was connected intimately with councils and endeavored to draw out implications for churches seeking unity in the twentieth century.

The Second Vatican Council was also causing Roman Catholic scholars to give increased consideration to reception. In 1970 the veteran patristic authority Aloys Grillmeier wrote on the topic of councils and reception.[13] He began by noting the importance that reception as related to synods or councils was gaining in ecumenical discussions. As theologians and churches took up this topic, they needed to be aware of the research done in Germany in the field of jurisprudence, where reception was seen as a centuries-long process whereby the legal system of the Roman Empire was received in the German legal system. Grillmeier accepted the conclusions of the legal historian Franz Wieacker that reception does not exist unless two different cultural areas are involved.[14] One takes over a law from the other. Thus genuine reception is exogenous, not endogenous; it is epidemic, not endemic. Wieacker traced out this legal reception as a process taking centuries and entailing the intellectual rationalizing of the whole of public life. Grillmeier turned to reception in the theological area, observing that until recently reception was a concern of canonists. He referred to the significant work in the last century by Rudolph Sohm, who defined reception as *recipere bonum aliquod*. According to Grillmeier, such research is important but ecumenical

12. Ibid., 98.

13. Aloys Grillmeier, "Konzil und Rezeption," *Theologie und Philosophie* 45 (1970): 320–53.

14. Franz Wieacker, *Privatrechtsgeschichte der Neuzeit unter besonderer Berücksichtigung der deutschen Entwicklung,* 2d ed. (Göttingen: Vandenhoeck & Ruprecht, 1967).

reflection on reception should not be so narrow. He examined the synods and councils of the early church to find examples of genuine and spurious reception involving both partner churches and churches separated from each other.

In this survey, Grillmeier identified a new point: mutual reception can become a central theme of ecumenical understanding. It is not merely an acceptance of texts and decisions of church teaching from one church by another but a living power of critical dialogue that should lead to unity in particulars and include Antioch, Alexandria, Constantinople, Wittenberg, Geneva, and Rome.[15]

Grillmeier discussed the various sorts of councils in the early church, showing how they relate to different understandings of the church. In moving to recent times, he saw the First Vatican Council as a council of the hierarchy. Behind this kind of council is a certain model of the church, where reception, at least for the laity, is merely passive obedience. From the hierarchy, and especially the pope, the hearing church of priests and faithful receives from the teaching church of bishops. Here is Wieacker's exogenous reception. The second partner receives from the first something it did not create. Grillmeier contrasts this with the Second Vatican Council, which presented and implied different views of the church and reception. He believed that this idea of reception has ecumenical promise. Reception must involve theologians, church leaders, and the faithful. A new interpretation of reception as removed from the narrow confines of canonists and as an exchange of spiritual goods, as a living process, can be expected by the churches. In remarkable ways, Grillmeier's article was ahead of its time, identifying aspects of reception that would become topics of debate fifteen years later.

Two years later, Yves Congar, the French Roman Catholic ecumenist, addressed many of the same topics as Grillmeier.[16] Congar found Wieacker's view of reception too narrow. He observed the new interest in reception in ecumenical circles but cautioned that church history contains an array of receptions and theories of reception. Con-

---

15. Grillmeier, "Konzil und Rezeption," 336–37.

16. Yves Congar, "La 'réception' comme réalité ecclésiologique," *Revue des sciences philosophiques et théologiques* 56 (1972): 500–514. Engl. trans.: "Reception as an Ecclesiological Reality," in *Election and Consensus in the Church,* ed. G. Alberigo and A. Weiler, Concilium 77 (New York: Herder & Herder, 1972), 43–68.

gar defined reception as a process by which a church acknowledges the measure it promulgates as a rule applicable to its own life.[17] He saw in the Second Vatican Council continuing interest in reception which can be traced back to the councils of Nicaea and Constantinople and to other councils of the early church and the West in the second millennium. He offered a historical review of patristic texts, indicating how councils of individual or local churches came, by reception, to be viewed as great councils of the entire church. Reception of any council's conclusions depended finally on whether or not the council was seen as transmitting the faith of the apostles.

Congar gave additional examples of reception. The canon of Scripture evolved by a process of reception. Liturgical texts and forms reached humanity by means of reception, as did law and discipline. Congar also offered illustrations of nonreception, among which he included the councils of Chalcedon and Florence, and the *filioque* clause.

In the section on theological interpretation, Congar, like Grillmeier, argued that the concept of reception must be freed from its association with constitutional law. It should be aligned with an ecclesiology that sees the whole body of the church, structured locally as individual churches, enlivened by the Holy Spirit. Underlying this ecclesiology are two conditions: (1) that the universal church cannot err in faith, and (2) that consensus is an effect of the Holy Spirit and the sign of the Spirit's presence. Congar insisted that reception did not confer validity but that it affirmed, acknowledged, and attested that the matter undergoing reception is good for the church—that it contains a decision ensuring the good of the church. Congar's treatment was not as directly connected to the immediate ecumenical situation as was Grillmeier's, but his careful historical review of reception furnished a significant resource for an advance in the discussion of this topic.

The ideas presented in both these articles found a forum for lively discussion when the World Council's Commission on Faith and Order met in Louvain in 1971. At this meeting Roman Catholic theologians took part for the first time as full members—one of the fruits of the Second Vatican Council. As both the study reports presented to the commission and the documents and reports from the meeting make

---

17. Congar, "Reception as an Ecclesiological Reality," 45.

clear, reception was entering the ecumenical vocabulary in a decisive way.[18] Once again reception was explored in the context of councils. This time it was viewed in connection with the Council of Chalcedon. The commission saw churches in the ecumenical movement to be in the process of the continuing reception or re-reception of the councils. This process raises questions about the reception or rejection of Chalcedon in the different traditions, about the present status of anathemas pronounced by the councils, and about the various concepts of tradition. The "study of the Council of Chalcedon" and "conciliarity and the future of the ecumenical movement" were to remain on the agenda of the Commission on Faith and Order. Both topics ensured that reception would also continue to receive attention.

Thus it has been possible to observe how the Second Vatican Council moved reception to the center of attention. As a direct result of the council, reception became a topic of ecumenical interest. This represented a recovery of interest in reception—in a concept and word that had dropped from theological discussion. The early renewal of interest, from 1960 until the mid-1970s, was largely characterized by concern with *conciliar* reception, and it looked back to the early church and to the Orthodox churches as resources. Yet this initial ecumenical attraction had more than a historical motivation. There was eagerness to see how reception could become a resource for enabling divided churches to move closer to unity. This is observable not only in World Council literature but in the writings of Roman Catholic theologians.

The Second Vatican Council was not, however, merely an event that called back reception for theological preoccupation. The council itself produced a number of significant documents requiring reception within the Roman Catholic church. As the Roman Catholic church has come to view itself as more collegial and to see reception as more than juridical decision, more attention has been given to how the conciliar documents are received within the church. It is recognized that reception is a process that goes on after a council itself finishes its work. Only twenty years have elapsed since the council. Reception of the Second Vatican Council's conclusions has been neither smooth nor

---

18. *Faith and Order: Louvain, 1971,* Faith and Order paper 59 (Geneva: World Council of Churches, 1971), 23–34, 224–29.

uniform in the Roman Catholic church. It is certainly not completed. The processes of reception or rejection, assimilation and actualization, of the council's conclusions within the Roman Catholic church will continue for many years. The twentieth anniversary of the council not only was the occasion for an extraordinary synod to take stock of the developments since the council but it prompted literature that examined the reception the council has encountered.[19] If for no other reason, such internal Roman Catholic attention to reception has an impact on the ecumenical movement because final reception of the Second Vatican Council's teachings will greatly influence the Roman Catholic church's future relations to ecumenism. An interest in Roman Catholics' reception of their own council contributes to the present fascination with reception.

There is one more reason for contemporary interest in reception. Reception returned to center stage in theological discussion not simply because the Second Vatican Council raised for the ecumenical movement an interest in councils but also because it authorized the entrance of the Roman Catholic church into that movement. It is no accident that ecumenical dialogues, or bilateral conversations, have proliferated since the 1960s. Theological discussions undertaken by officially appointed representatives of two churches, two traditions or confessional families, with purposes ranging from promoting mutual understanding to achieving full fellowship have occurred in the ecumenical movement for years.[20] Within the last twenty-five years they have assumed a special importance. The earlier ecumenical activities allowed the churches to overcome animosities and build trust. Insights of biblical and patristic scholarship were becoming more widely accepted within the churches. It was becoming possible to look at earlier theological disagreements and historical events in new ways. But a major reason for the great increase in dialogue activity in the past twenty-five years has been the involvement of the Roman Catholic church. With its resources and size, that church has had a considerable effect on the dialogues that it authorized as a result of the work of the Second Vatican Council. The dialogues that Roman

19. See, e.g., *La réception de Vatican II,* ed. G. Alberigo and J. P. Jossua (Paris: Editions du Cerf, 1985).

20. Nils Ehrenström and Günther Gassmann, *Confessions in Dialogue,* 3d ed., Faith and Order paper 74 (Geneva: World Council of Churches, 1975), 10.

Catholics have had with Anglicans and Lutherans and with the Orthodox and Reformed traditions have in turn had their influence on the dialogues those churches have conducted among themselves. At the same time the numerous dialogues involving the Roman Catholic church could not help being influenced by the other conversations. The past twenty-five years have witnessed an increase in dialogues and a demonstrable interrelation between them.

Two volumes illustrate both of these points clearly. Nils Ehrenström and Günther Gassmann in *Confessions in Dialogue*[21] and Harding Meyer and Lukas Vischer in *Growth in Agreement*[22] document the upsurge in dialogue activity. Even if one surveys only bilateral conversations on the world level, the increase can be demonstrated. Since 1970 there have been reports from Anglican-Lutheran conversations, Anglican-Orthodox conversations, Anglican–Roman Catholic conversations, Baptist-Reformed conversations, Lutheran–Roman Catholic conversations, Methodist–Roman Catholic conversations, and Reformed–Roman Catholic conversations. This list, although not exhaustive, is impressive. As would be expected, the reports of these dialogues have considerable variation, yet one common motif runs through most of them. They ask the churches who sponsor the conversations to take some action, to receive the results of the dialogues, and to be changed by that action. In short, the dialogues request the churches to be engaged in what is now commonly understood as reception.

In a particularly concrete way, the international Anglican–Roman Catholic dialogue is now engaging its sponsoring churches in the task of evaluating the dialogue's work, examining its claimed agreements, and exploring the implications. The various churches of the Anglican communion, and the Roman Catholic church in its dioceses and at the Vatican, are preparing responses to the dialogue. All this activity must be seen as part of what is involved in reception. The Anglican–Roman Catholic dialogue had its beginning in 1966. The need for evaluation of its work was recognized in the Common Declaration of Pope Paul

21. See n. 20.

22. Harding Meyer and Lukas Vischer, eds., *Growth in Agreement: Reports and Agreements of Ecumenical Conversations on a World Level* (New York and Ramsey, N.J.: Paulist Press, 1984). Original, German ed.: *Dokumente wachsender Übereinstimmung* (Paderborn: Verlag Bonifatius-Druckerei, 1983).

VI and Donald Coggan, archbishop of Canterbury, in 1977.[23] The present evaluation process shows that the response of the Sacred Congregation for the Doctrine of Faith, of 1982, should not be regarded as the final word of the Roman Catholic church to this dialogue.[24]

The Lutheran–Roman Catholic dialogue has also issued reports urging conclusions upon its sponsoring churches. From the first report, the Malta Report, in 1972, this dialogue has called upon the churches to evaluate its work and to enter into a "special life process" together.[25] The concluding section of the report *The Eucharist* of 1978 is entitled "Reception." It notes that a theological teaching remains a theory as long as it is not affirmed and adopted by the whole people of God. It asks the dialogue participants and fellow Christians to examine, improve, and make their own the work of the dialogue.[26] The document on ministry, of 1981, in discussing future possibilities has suggested to the churches that the only way to solve the issue of ministry is through a process in which the churches "reciprocally accept each other"—through, that is, reception.[27] The most recent document from this dialogue, *Facing Unity*, asks the churches to examine, perhaps correct and supplement, and finally give authority to, the dialogue's conclusions.[28] Here is another example of a dialogue requesting reception. Although the Lutheran World Federation has asked its member churches for reactions to the dialogue, and although opinions have been sought within the Roman Catholic church, the process of reception is less advanced here than it is with the Anglican–Roman Catholic dialogue.

Additional examples could be given. The international Disciples–Roman Catholic conversations in 1981 concluded their report by asking both churches to enter to the fullest extent possible into a process of mutual recognition[29] that, obviously, requires reception of the

23. Meyer and Vischer, eds., *Growth in Agreement*, 127.

24. "Observations on the ARCIC Final Report," *Origins* 11 (1982): 752–56.

25. Meyer and Vischer, eds., *Growth in Agreement*, 168, 186; and *Lutheran World* 19 (1972): 259, 271.

26. Meyer and Vischer, eds., *Growth in Agreement*, 212; and *The Eucharist* (Geneva: Lutheran World Federation, 1980), 28.

27. Meyer and Vischer, eds., *Growth in Agreement*, 273; and *The Ministry in the Church* (Geneva: Lutheran World Federation, 1982), 31.

28. *Facing Unity* (Geneva: Lutheran World Federation, 1985), 6. German ed.: *Einheit vor uns* (Paderborn: Verlag Bonifatius-Druckerei, 1986).

29. Meyer and Vischer, eds., *Growth in Agreement*, 165–66.

dialogue's conclusions. Among the regional dialogues, of special note are the European conversations involving Lutheran, Reformed, and United churches. These conversations led to the Leuenberg Agreement of 1971, which was submitted to the European Reformation churches. The agreement was revised and completed at a further session at Leuenberg in 1973 and sent to the churches for approval by September 30, 1974.[30] It proposed church fellowship by the way of concord, church fellowship based on the consensus reached in an understanding of the gospel, so that churches with different confessional positions might accord each other fellowship in Word and Sacrament. The agreement resulted in intense debates, but a number of churches declared their assent. Thus this agreement marks one of the few times that dialogue has led its participating churches to enter into a process of reception.

The European Anglican-Lutheran dialogue placed a series of recommendations at the conclusion of its report, proposing interim steps by which the churches could move to full communion. For the churches to take these steps, they must be prepared to identify with the conclusions of Anglican-Lutheran dialogues—to receive them.[31]

In the United States, both national and regional discussions have invited reception by the churches. The Lutheran-Episcopal dialogue in 1973 produced the proposal of intercommunion between the churches.[32] In 1981, the second series of dialogues between Episcopalians and Lutherans asked the churches to recognize each other as true churches and to work out a policy of interim eucharistic hospitality.[33] In 1982, three of the sponsoring Lutheran churches along with the Episcopal Church in the USA entered into an agreement based on the dialogue work but not at one in every detail with the dialogue's proposals. This step is the only example until now in the United States of reception of a dialogue's achievements, and it is a partial reception.

---

30. "Agreement (*Konkordie*) among Reformation Churches in Europe," *Ecumenical Review* 25 (1973): 355–59; James E. Andrews and Joseph A. Burgess, eds., *An Invitation to Action: The Lutheran-Reformed Dialogue, Series III* (Philadelphia: Fortress Press, 1984), 61–73; and *Lutheran World* 20 (1973): 347–53.

31. *Anglican-Lutheran Dialogue: The Report of the European Regional Commission* (London: SPCK, 1983), 29–33.

32. *Lutheran-Episcopal Dialogue: A Progress Report* (Cincinnati: Forward Movement Pubs., 1973).

33. *Lutheran-Episcopal Dialogue: The Report of the Lutheran-Episcopal Dialogue, Second Series, 1976–1980* (Cincinnati: Forward Movement Pubs., 1981).

The step involved not just official convention actions of the four churches but an overwhelming positive response to the agreement on the part of the local churches.[34] The third series of Lutheran-Reformed dialogues, in 1983, specifically requested the churches of both traditions to enter into a process of reception so that the conclusions of the dialogue might become part of the faith and life of the churches.[35] The most recent common statement from the Lutheran–Roman Catholic dialogue in the United States, *Justification by Faith*, published in 1984, closed with a declaration which the dialogue members submitted to their churches in the obvious hope of some positive response.[36]

A final example of the call for reception that has resulted from theological conversations between divided churches comes not from bilateral dialogues but from the multilateral discussions of the Faith and Order movement. In 1982 the Commission on Faith and Order published the document *Baptism, Eucharist and Ministry*.[37] This text was produced after some fifty-five years of work. Heavily indebted to bilateral dialogues, *Baptism, Eucharist and Ministry* claims an ecumenical convergence on three crucial ecumenical subjects. More than one hundred theologians from a great variety of traditions considered this text to have reached a stage of sufficient maturity that they transmitted it to their churches, asking them to do two things. The churches were requested to take up the question of reception involving the whole people of God and all levels of church life. This was seen as a long-term process, requiring commitment to a long-term goal. The churches were also asked to prepare an official response to *Baptism, Eucharist and Ministry* at their highest level of authority. Response was carefully distinguished from the process of reception.[38] The distinction will be discussed in the final chapter of this book.

By 1978, even before the publication of *Baptism, Eucharist and*

---

34. See *The Lutheran-Episcopal Agreement: Commentary and Guidelines* (New York: Division for World Mission and Ecumenism, Lutheran Church in America, 1983).

35. Andrews and Burgess, eds., *Invitation to Action*, 5.

36. H. George Anderson, T. Austin Murphy, and Joseph A. Burgess, eds., *Justification by Faith: Lutherans and Catholics in Dialogue VII* (Minneapolis: Augsburg Pub. House, 1985), esp. 73–74.

37. *Baptism, Eucharist and Ministry*, Faith and Order paper 111 (Geneva: World Council of Churches, 1982).

38. Ibid., x.

Ministry, the Commission on Faith and Order was turning its attention to reception as it was emerging from the various dialogues. In that year the commission held a forum with various Christian world communions, in order to facilitate the exchange of information about the dialogues, to promote an interaction between bilateral and multilateral discussions, and to study the implications of the dialogues for the whole ecumenical movement. This meeting led to two other sessions, held in 1979 and 1980.[39]

The first forum, in 1978, dealt chiefly with concepts of unity but spoke briefly as well to the topic of reception. In a subsection entitled "The Process of Reception of the Results of the Dialogues," the forum declared that reception is the responsibility of the churches and that the publication of the dialogues' work is an intentional part of the reception process. The forum also suggested that a process of several stages needs to be developed and that in the future new methodologies and the use of a broader range of expertise and analyses will be needed.[40] These comments, modest in character, are evidence all the same that requests for the reception of the dialogues' work are being heard.

The second forum, in 1979, did not take up the subject of reception directly, but the report "How Does the Church Teach Authoritatively Today?" from the Commission on Faith and Order did.[41] This report acknowledged the need for a stronger emphasis on the reception of teachings by the whole church. To the degree that teachings have been arrived at by the involvement of all the faithful, reception is facilitated. Reception, according to the report, is not to be understood as just involving decisions arranged from above that are submitted to the community for passive reception. Involving more than official endorsement, reception is a profound appropriation, through a gradual testing, by which teachings are made part of the life and liturgy of the community.[42] Although these remarks are not directly related to a

---

39. *The Three Reports of the Forum on Bilateral Conversations*, Faith and Order paper 107 (Geneva: World Council of Churches, 1980).

40. Ibid., 7; and Daniel F. Martensen, "The Federation and the World Council of Churches," *LWF Report* 3 (1978): 58–59.

41. *How Does the Church Teach Authoritatively Today?* Faith and Order paper 91 (Geneva: World Council of Churches, 1979).

42. Ibid., 88.

discussion of the dialogues, there is little question that this whole study is connected with the advance achieved in the theological conversations.[43]

The forum of 1980 devoted a major portion of its report to reception.[44] The dramatic increase in just two years documents the growing preoccupation with this topic. The report indicated the various meanings of reception—as, for example, an acceptance of the decision of a council and (the more comprehensive meaning) a process by which a church makes the results of a dialogue its own. Also recognized were the various levels and forms of reception. And the belief that reception ultimately occurs as Christ graciously accomplishes it by his Spirit-reception was acknowledged as more than an intellectual exercise. Reception is a spiritual process of communication within the church that is both dynamic and dialogical. New understandings rather than imposition of one's own beliefs are involved. Reception of joint statements is not an end in itself but always a step on the way toward fuller visible unity. This process is incomplete until not just the consent of the members of the *koinonia* is arrived at but their true commitment.

Although not necessarily envisioned in the initial series of meetings, a fourth forum met in 1985.[45] The report of the forum provides an updating of dialogue activities since 1980, including the publication of some reactions to *Baptism, Eucharist and Ministry*. A major part of the report is entitled "Emerging Features in the Response/Reception Process."[46] Here some of the insights gained from the recent discussions of reception are noted. Response and reception are distinguished and seen as part of an ongoing process. Responses by the churches to *Baptism, Eucharist and Ministry* and to the dialogues are not the same as the reception of their perspectives into the life of the churches. Response is an early step in the process that is reception. Both response and reception are viewed as opportunities for renewal. It is noted that the churches are being asked to reply to too many dialogue

---

43. Ibid., 78.

44. *Three Reports of the Forum*, 38–44; and Daniel F. Martensen, "LWF Ecumenical Relations in Review: 1980," *LWF Documentation* 7 (1981): 10–14.

45. *The Report of the Fourth Forum on Bilateral Conversations*, Faith and Order paper 125 (Geneva: World Council of Churches, 1985).

46. Ibid., 14–16.

reports too quickly. More time is needed, for the challenge is one not only of doctrinal and pastoral reflection but of the embodiment of the interim results of the dialogues in action. Opportunities are to be sought to turn agreements in doctrine into common worship, witness, and service.

In all these examples from the dialogues and from the Commission on Faith and Order, we observe a push to a phase where the goal is no longer convergence or consensus but the translation of theological agreements into practice in a living fellowship of churches, that is, reception. The phases of convergence, consensus, and reception overlap, and the challenge of the immediate future will be to shift our concentration to more concrete attempts to convert agreements into fellowship. In support of these attempts, decisions must be made, where appropriate, to give agreements the kind of authoritative character in the churches that will advance ecclesial fellowship.

Under pressure from the dialogues, the meaning of reception has shifted or at least expanded. John Zizioulas has spoken of the "classical idea of reception" and the present ecumenical situation.[47] For our immediate purposes it may be useful to build on his vocabulary and speak about "classical reception" and "ecumenical reception." Classical reception is reception as it was understood before the rise of the modern ecumenical movement; ecumenical reception is reception as it is understood since the increase of ecumenical dialogue during the 1960s. Although there are similarities between the two concepts of reception, there are also significant differences.

The classical idea of reception is mainly associated with councils of the church and their decisions. From this association, the word "reception" entered into the terminology of canon law, where it was used primarily for the acceptance and consent given by the faithful to a particular conciliar or ecclesiastical decision. Such acceptance often occurred with remarkable simplicity and might require no juridically normative bodies apart from those already functioning in a spiritual and pastoral manner, namely, synods of bishops. There were of course instances in the early church where reception was not so straightforward, but the early church was a united church whose organs of reception were known and acknowledged. In the early

47. John Zizioulas, "The Theological Problem of Reception," *Centro pro Unione Bulletin* 26 (1984): 4–6.

church one also sees local churches receive from one another. Even if verbal confessions or creeds were involved, there was an understanding that in the final analysis what was received was the gospel itself. In this process, not individuals but churches as communities were the active participants. For the early church this meant that the local bishop played a key but not independent role in the community's decision. In including the local churches, reception always had a universal dimension and needed the concurrence of the church catholic. Nevertheless, the early church allowed freedom of expression and different cultural forms in reception. There were varying liturgies, texts of prayers, and formulations of doctrine, but such variety did not preclude reception. Rather, it enriched the entire church.

Now, classical reception has some notable differences from ecumenical reception. The context of ecumenical reception is not one united church; instead, there are separated churches that are called to receive from one another. In this setting what is sought is not simply agreement in doctrine but mutual ecclesial reception. This raises numerous questions about the continuity of individual churches with the past, about the identification of the appropriate organs within these bodies for reception, and about how reception is possible within an incomplete or broken eucharistic community. For the first time, churches are being asked to receive materials they did not directly produce. Ecumenical reception involves a fundamental sharing in the one apostolic faith as it has been handed down in many communities of faith. The church communities are now struggling to reinterpret their common heritage with new language, new emphases, and new insights, all acquired by participation in the one ecumenical movement. This kind of reception must take account of converging elements that the separated church communities can confess together because the elements have been found in dialogue to meet in the one apostolic faith. Ecumenical reception forces churches to come to grips with painful questions that have divided them for centuries. It is not difficult to see why reception of this nature represents a major challenge to the churches. As Dom Emmanuel Lane reminded the meeting of the Commission on Faith and Order in Lima when he spoke about the ecumenical reception of *Baptism, Eucharist and Ministry*, "It is also essential that all the churches should see that their reception of this document concern them at the very centre of their being. What is at stake here is the full communion which they desire to recover and the visible unity to which they are called."[48]

We can now develop at least a preliminary definition of the term "ecumenical reception." The preliminary character of the definition must be underscored, for ecumenical reception is still a reality of which we have but an initial and partial experience.[49] Nevertheless, we can define it to include *all phases and aspects of an ongoing process by which a church under the guidance of God's Spirit makes the results of a bilateral or multilateral conversation a part of its faith and life because the results are seen to be in conformity with the teachings of Christ and of the apostolic community, that is, the gospel as witnessed to in Scripture.*

This tentative formulation recognizes that ecumenical agreements have come from outside the separate participating churches and have made claims on them. It acknowledges that the question put by ecumenical reception before all the churches is the degree to which they are prepared to make authoritative within their own life the conclusions of ecumenical dialogue. Examples of such reception are still rare. The Leuenberg Agreement in Europe, the Lutheran-Episcopal Agreement in the United States, and the action of some churches in the United States to the Lutheran-Reformed dialogue are among the few illustrations of even partial reception.

Before concluding this discussion, I want to give at least brief attention to another area where reception has come to be hotly debated: that of literary studies.[50] A method of literary criticism—and, when it is applied to the Bible, of hermeneutic criticism—has been developed

---

48. Michael Kinnamon, ed., *Towards Visible Unity: Commission on Faith and Order, Lima, 1982,* vol. 1, Faith and Order paper 112 (Geneva: World Council of Churches, 1982), 53.

49. As recently as 1984, declared Monsignor Richard Steward ("'Reception': What Do the Churches Do with Ecumenical Agreements?" *Centro pro Unione Bulletin* 25 [1984]: 2), he had met a person who refused to define reception in a paper because the reality did not completely exist.

50. I am indebted to Carol Thysell, a graduate student at the University of Chicago and a former consultant to the Commission on Faith and Order of the National Council of Churches of Christ in the USA, for reminding me of the reception theory in literary criticism. The literature in this area is vast. Two useful starting places, valuable also for their bibliographies, are Edgar V. McKnight's *The Bible and the Reader: An Introduction to Literary Criticism* (Philadelphia: Fortress Press, 1985) and Bernard C. Lategan and William S. Vorster's *Text and Reality: Aspects of Reference in Biblical Texts* (Philadelphia: Fortress Press, 1985).

in which the reader is deliberately included in the process of interpretation and analysis. Here the very reality of a literary work is considered to be dependent on comprehension by a reader. Thus attention is given to what happens on the receiving side in communication and to what role the reader plays in determining the meaning of a text. Questions have been raised about whether a text has any existence apart from its reception by its readers and about whether a text has one or several possible meanings. Reception is seen as an existential event implying an individual and personal decision regarding the meaning of the text. As a result, texts are seen as having trajectories that are determined by the extended process of reception and reinterpretation during their histories.

There appears to be no direct connection between the theory of reception in literary criticism and the discussion now being carried on in ecumenical theology. Nevertheless, to be inattentive to literary criticism here could impoverish ecumenical thinking about reception, for some parallels do exist between the two discussions. Both are concerned about written texts and about how readers (individuals or churches) understand and finally receive the texts existentially so that both receptors and texts are changed.

Our description in this chapter has raised some issues that seem very old and others that seem very new. Aspects of reception involving the canon of Scripture and decisions of councils are rooted in the first centuries of Christian existence. Other dimensions of reception, such as those concerning the acceptance of ecumenical dialogues, have a history no longer than two or three decades. We must now step back from the current situation and observe in some detail the history of reception in the church.

2

A HISTORY
OF RECEPTION

In the previous chapter we described recent discussion concerning reception. This allowed us to see reception as an important topic in contemporary ecumenical reflection. In this chapter we shall try to place reception in a broader historical perspective than our passing references to earlier stages of church history have afforded. This will permit us in the final chapter to offer suggestions for an ecumenical vision of reception for the future.

Others have already said that reception precedes the church itself.[1] It is certainly true in a sense that the church arose out of a continuing process of reception. Thus in the Old Testament it is possible to discern the motifs of receiving and re-receiving. For example, creation itself receives its being from its creator God. It is only as human beings receive the revelation of God that they know God's presence. Israel receives its existence by the election and covenant of God. It receives the promised land and responds by worship and praise. Individuals within Israel receive the title of servant of God. In the Old Testament there is evidence of the ongoing process of giving and receiving from God that at least partly answers Israel's need to receive continually and, in an utter dependence on God, to re-receive God's gifts of mercy and love. See, for example, Genesis 1, Exodus 19—24, Deuteronomy 7, Jeremiah 2, and Isaiah 34.

It is this environment that is the birthplace of Jesus of Nazareth. The New Testament makes clear that he receives his mission from his heavenly Father, and his place and context as a human being from the history of Israel (Matthew 1—4; Mark 1; Luke 2—4). Thus the Lord of

---

1. See John Zizioulas, "The Theological Problem of Reception," *Centro pro Unione Bulletin* 26 (1984): 3.

the church receives before his church receives from him. The New Testament also clearly shows that the community of faith receives from Christ. In the parable of the sower, it is the word that is accepted (Mark 4:20). Later in Mark, Jesus tells his disciples that whoever does not receive the kingdom of God as a child will not enter it (Mark 10:15). The idea of receiving Christ as the Word plays an important role in the first chapter of the Gospel according to John. This is true especially in vv. 11 and 12, where it is stated that his own received him not, but that to all who received and believed was given the power to become children of God. In Acts, those who accept the preaching of Peter, the message of Jesus, are subsequently baptized (Acts 2:41). The same book speaks of the apostles, the brethren, and Jews, as receiving the Word (Acts 8:14; 11:1; 17:11). Other texts indicate that the disciples and messengers of Jesus are received (Matt. 10:40; John 13:20). Acts 15 is extremely significant, because, although what is reported there is idealized, it gives a description of an ecclesial reception process. The decision of the apostolic council of Jerusalem is transmitted by messengers to the church in Antioch. The church there rejoices at the decision. Although the word "receive" or "accept" is not used, the validity of the so-called apostles' decree is confirmed by reception.

The notion of reception is present not only in the Gospels and Acts. Paul recalls for the Corinthians that they have received the Gospel he preached (1 Cor. 15:1). In like manner, he tells them that they have received the Holy Spirit (1 Cor. 2:12; cf. 1 Thess. 2:13 and Col. 2:6). Paul reminds the Romans that those accepted by Christ are to accept one another (Rom. 15:7). Reception regarding the process of tradition is also referred to in Pauline passages. Paul introduces the accounts of the institution of the Lord's supper with technical rabbinic terms denoting a process of tradition reception (1 Cor. 11:23). Several times Paul uses *paradidonai* and *paralambanein*, the Greek equivalents for the rabbinic terms, for a process of handing-on and receiving the tradition. In this reception of tradition is included an interpretation of what is received. The message of God contained in the tradition is applied with special force to the contemporary moment.

This practice appears to be reflected throughout the New Testament and not just in the Pauline corpus; see, for example, John 14:17; 15:26; 16:13; Matt. 18:20; 28:20; 1 John 5:6; 1 Tim. 3:15; Eph. 5:9. Often the words "receive" and "accept" are not used but the concepts involved in the words are. One thing is clear throughout the New Testament: what is really important is the Lord himself and what he gives in word and deed. What is accepted has its own intrinsic authority. It is a new and special thing to each situation, and those addressed are able neither to stand in judgment over what has been given nor to add to its content. All they can do is make room for it in and around themselves, and even in this situation it is the Spirit that gives the basis for understanding and receiving things that are of the Spirit. Such New Testament texts may reveal an early, certainly presynodal practice of reception in the life of early Christian congregations.

Despite differences of detail, the various books of the New Testament describe a process of reception that is not legal and formal but a glad process of receiving the good news of the gospel, and indeed of the Lord himself. This is always an event of the Holy Spirit. In this biblical sense, reception is one of the main characteristics of the faith itself. Christians believe they receive the body and blood of Christ through the bread and wine of the Lord's Supper, as they receive their mission to be disciples, ministers, prophets, and teachers. This is why when the Bible speaks of reception it is addressing the heart of a receiving faith. What occurred as a result of the reception of this apostolic preaching by those who became the converts of the apostles and the other early Christian missionaries was quite simply the church itself. The church is the end product of the reception process portrayed in the Bible.

Thus the church first receives from God through Christ in the Spirit as it also receives its context from the world, history, and culture. Then the church is received as a distinct community in the world with which it must be in constant dialogue and as one church is received by other churches. For in the New Testament the church as one exists as churches and these churches exist as the one church in and through receiving one another as sister churches. In this process not just the leadership of the churches is active but all the people of God.

This is all closely connected with what is being received in the New Testament view. In the final analysis it is the incarnate Son given by the Father in the Spirit. Or as Paul often puts it, the church receives not only Christ but the gospel, this good news of God's love for the world. Thus the church receives the historical facts about Jesus Christ.

These facts may be passed on by verbal confessions, but this should not remove the personal-existence character from reception as described in Scripture. The church receives above all a person and is received in turn as the body of that person, Christ.[2]

Obviously from what has been said, reception is a rich biblical concept. It is often presented without the use of the word "receive" or "accept" in Scripture. Thus the study of reception in the Bible should not be limited to a word study. Yet it is useful to observe that in the New Testament, reception is expressed mainly through the two verbs *lambanein* and *dechesthai. Lambanein* and related words like *apolambanein* are used rather more explicitly for the active grasping hold of what is given and comes to human beings. *Dechesthai* and related words like *apodechesthai, doche,* and *apodoche* are employed with greater variation. The subjective factors and valuations on the part of the person receiving are included. These involve glad and reverent acceptance, inner assimilation, and practical adoption. Thus although the two sets of words are not exactly synonymous, the former having the more passive sense of receiving and the latter the meaning of accepting, the New Testament consistently affirms that he who is received and accepted is none other than Jesus the Christ.

As we move from the New Testament period into that of the early church, some changes begin to become obvious. *First Clement* 58.2 speaks of receiving "our symbol," and in Ignatius of Antioch, for example, *Magn.* 13.1 talks of being confirmed in the ordinances of the Lord and the apostles. Indeed there are hints of such ideas within the New Testament—for instance, in Heb. 13:9 and Col. 2:7—but in the apostolic fathers reception is linked with a manner of intellectual and spiritual acceptance that is much less personal and that is a matter of consolidating what has already been given.

In the pre-Constantinian period reception was concerned primarily with the process by which local and regional synods were made known and accepted by other churches. The operating presupposition was that a particular church was authentically the church only as it lived in communion with other churches. The early church saw itself as a fellowship of churches involved in the process of giving and taking from one another. According to the belief of the church,

---

2. See a useful summary of many of these ideas in ibid., 4–5.

each synod, irrespective of its size, had the Holy Spirit. Although all churches were recognized as able to speak for the whole church, this conciliar authority was based on two factors: (1) the known orthodoxy of the participants, and (2) ultimately, the ability of the council to call forth reception from the churches. Aloys Grillmeier in his article on reception devotes some attention to these local councils.[3] Actually, considerable attention has been given to the history of these synods, but specific examination of the factors and phases by which any council came to be regarded as ecumenical is still needed. Nevertheless, several characteristics emerge from the preliminary research that has been conducted. For example, when what is to be received already exists in a vital way in the original resources of faith of the receiving community, the process of reception is quicker and easier. Familiar ideas of faith and practice do not present the problems of strange suggestions. Also—and this follows upon the first characteristic—reception occurs through a more or less complicated process. Grillmeier traces out this process for the Council of Chalcedon—admittedly not a local council—in the Roman Catholic church.[4] One sees at once how many stages were involved in the final reception. Finally, in all the instances of reception there is an understanding that what is being accomplished is not merely a juridical action of acceptance by church officials. Rather, the juridical action is seen as beginning a spiritual process of reception by the entire community in which the episcopal office assures that the reception is in conformity with the earliest Christian communities and that it is in common with the other ecclesial communities in the world.

Numerous examples of local synods could be reviewed. Synods met in Asia Minor in the second century to deal with Montanism. These gatherings acted in the belief that the apostolic word and spirit exist within the church, so they decreed with authority and often their resolutions were accepted outside their areas. In the third century, synods were often called in Egypt and North Africa as well as in Asia Minor. A factor contributing to this development was the evolving theology of episcopacy. The bishop was seen as not only the head of

---

3. Aloys Grillmeier, "Konzil and Rezeption," *Theologie und Philosophie* 45 (1970): 331–37.

4. Aloys Grillmeier, "The Reception of Chalcedon in the Roman Catholic Church," *Ecumenical Review* 22 (1970): 383–411.

the local gathering but the voice of his local church in relation to other churches. Bishops in councils were assembled with increasing frequency. Early councils of bishops began to gather in the year 190 because of the paschal controversy. Eusebius is a major source for information about such synods (*Ecclesiastical History* 5.24–25, 34). According to him, councils were convoked in Italy, Gaul, and Corinth. All these gatherings were local, chaired by a bishop, and assigned importance according to the number of participants as well as to the achievement of unanimity, and they all had a purpose related to the Eucharist or Communion. Often conciliar letters were composed at the conclusion of the council and sent to the other churches. By the time of Cyprian, in the middle of the third century, regional councils (usually comprising bishops of a Roman province) were convoked at the metropolitan city of the area. The pattern was political, built on the model of the Roman senate. For Cyprian, the council was the expression of the unity of the episcopate, a unity based on the thought that all bishops possessed the one seat of Peter so that each local church was fully apostolic. The notion that each bishop had to express his unity with other bishops by taking part in a council was a step toward the idea of a larger council, but the execution of that idea was some years away.

One local council of greater importance than some others was the Synod of Antioch that met in the year 268. This local synod, which gathered in the East, was received by the churches of the East and West. It presented a clear example of the kind of authority that a local council could exercise within the one communion of churches. This local gathering condemned Paul of Samosata, who was supposed to have used the word *homoousios* to describe the relation of the Word to the Father (Eusebius *Ecclesiastical History* 7.30). When the Council of Nicaea some fifty-seven years later employed the very term *homoousios* in its confession of faith about the relation of the Son to the Father, the authority of the Synod of Antioch was so great that the supporters of Nicaea had to defend its condemnation of Paul's use of the word. Athanasius did this by insisting that the members of the Synod of Antioch were orthodox and handed on the divine tradition. The word *homoousios* had to be seen in its historical context (Athanasius *De synodis* 3). The Synod of Antioch is a vivid illustration of the reception of a local council's decisions by the entire church so that they could not be ignored. This reception was in agreement with the synod's own understanding of itself. Like other councils before Nicaea, Antioch was undergirded by the belief that each church as truly church was able to speak to other churches and for other churches. It is the same Spirit who guides the decisions of all the churches since they all live from the same Spirit. Similar notions were held by the Council of Arles, which met in 314. It could be assumed that even bishops absent from the council would speak in unison with those present, because it was the body of Christ that had gathered.[5] Thus in this period the decisions reached by local synods were made known to other churches by means of synodal letters and accepted by those churches.

In these processes the role of formal juridical acts is relatively minor. Seen as a whole, reception in these ante-Nicene councils is conceived as a spiritual and theological process of confirmation and completion. Even if there is a certain narrowness compared with the breadth of reception found in the New Testament, it is the wider framework of a spiritual event of transmission and acceptance that provides the key to the conception of reception operating in local and regional councils before the year 325.

As with so many things in the early church, with reception too, Constantine forms the dividing line. Pre- and post-Constantinian concepts of reception show some divergences. The original intention of Constantine's intervention in church affairs may well have been to allow the church to settle its own questions. There may indeed have been a parallelism in his mind between himself as the head of the empire, on the one hand, and the bishops summoned to a council as the head of Christ's empire, on the other. Bishops assembled as a court to deal with thorny issues could be a way out for an emperor with little theological background.[6] Nevertheless, the emperor's action had a profound influence. Councils were no longer concerned with the preservation of sacramental communion in the church but were now concerned with deciding questions of faith that affect the peace and security of the empire. Decisions of councils were no longer merely shared by synodical letter for church approval but were accepted

5. Grillmeier, "Konzil und Rezeption," 333 n. 33, 334 n. 34.
6. See John Zizioulas, "Development of Conciliar Structures in the Time of the First Ecumenical Council," *Councils and the Ecumenical Movement,* World Council of Churches Studies 5 (Geneva: World Council of Churches, 1968), 48–49.

directly by the emperor and acquired the status of imperial law. In theory, councils did have a freedom when assembled, but the deep involvement of the emperor in the conciliar process resulted in a cooperation between him and the bishops assembled. This fact aided the development of a new and critical phase in reception, in which the critical question became whether the council in its acts was obedient to the truth of faith. The church of the fourth century and later shows that the critical acceptance of a council's work was a theological process of decision in the life of the church, a process in which the laity, monks, and church leadership participated to an astonishing degree, with an enthusiasm that would seem strange to many today. Acceptance of a council's achievements was not simply a matter of imperial reception.

The Council of Nicaea of 325 provides one good example of this. Its decisions were received only after some fifty-six years of quarrels punctuated by synods, excommunications, exiles, imperial intervention, and violence. Synods in Tyre and Jerusalem ten years later rehabilitated Arius and deposed Athanasius. Even the Roman pope Julius did not seem certain that the decisions of Nicaea were irrevocable. Only the Council of Constantinople in 381 ended these disputes, but this council owes its claim to be ecumenical not to its composition but to the reception of its creed by the later Council of Chalcedon. Roman acceptance of the Council of Constantinople of 381 as the second of the first four ecumenical councils had to wait until the sixth century and Pope Hormisdas. The Council of Ephesus, in 431, met in circumstances that did not help its claim to be ecumenical. Cyril of Alexandria rushed through a decision before the arrival of bishops from Syria. Only later agreements between Cyril (and his followers) and John of Antioch (and his supporters) gave Ephesus some right to the title "ecumenical." In 451 the Council of Chalcedon received the writings of Pope Leo and two letters of Cyril along with the creeds of Nicaea and Constantinople, but the reception of Chalcedon's decisions became itself a long story with many explanations. There was a nonreception of the decisions on the part of the Armenian and Coptic churches. In contrast to this, the Third Council of Constantinople, in 681, received almost immediate confirmation in the West when Pope Leo II approved the council and asked the Spanish bishops to support it, and when they did so at the regional

Council of Toledo XIV, in 684. On the other hand, the decisions of the Second Council of Nicaea, in 787, had to wait many years before gaining acceptance in the West. Admittedly, bad translations of texts and political rivalry were all part of the story, but it was not until 1053 that there was an express reception of the work of the Second Council of Nicaea by the popes.

Thus it can be observed that in the period after Constantine, reception was seen as a process through which those decisions made by the great ecumenical councils were discussed, interpreted, and accepted by a later council. We have noted that reception did not occur in all cases. There was always the possibility of nonreception. In the period from 325 to 787 a variety of views about reception and the authority of the councils found expression. Hermann Josef Sieben has identified one consistent position that was determined by the ideas of *consensio antiquitatis* and *consensio universitatis.* Three theological aspects of the conciliar self-understanding of a universal council are included in that position. First, the council saw itself as having a high measure of authority and as being the mediator of the twofold consensus in the Spirit's power. Second, the importance of the reception of the council's decisions by the whole church was consequently brought into prominence. Finally, in view of the claim of the council, the assembly was regarded as bound to the teaching and preaching of Scripture as it was handed down in the church.[7] Sieben's work discloses that such councils were a risky business. They had to document a consensus of the entire church at a moment in history, the *consensio universitatis,* and at the same time demonstrate the *consensio antiquitatis.* The latter requirement limited the options of the councils: whatever they taught required a demonstrable consensus with Scripture and its preaching in the church. The *consensio antiquitatis* had also to be confirmed by reception. We have seen that the success of any council was determined not so much by the formal juridical authority that could be claimed as by the contents of the council's decision. There is evidence in the survey of councils we have already given that of the two kinds of consensus, *antiquitatis* and

7. Hermann Josef Sieben, *Die Konzilsidee der Alten Kirche,* Konzilen-Geschichte series B, Untersuchungen (Paderborn: Schöningh, 1979), 511–16; and Edward J. Kilmartin's summary "Reception in History," in *The Search for Visible Unity,* ed. Jeffrey Gros (New York: Pilgrim Press, 1984), 48–50.

universitatis, the former enjoyed a position of priority over the latter. A council that could not substantiate that it stood with the consensus of antiquity would have little chance of reception. That is because of the early church's understanding that the truth of faith is of its essence, a truth traditioned, that is, handed on. Acceptance of councils from the fourth century onward had a complexity far beyond simple imperial or papal endorsement.

Reception in the patristic church was taking place in areas besides that of the decisions of councils. One of the most notable of these is the area of liturgy. As the great liturgical traditions of the Eastern and Western churches were established, an extensive exchange of liturgical practices occurred. The exchange was facilitated by the view that all the local churches held the same faith and so had gifts to share with one another. The exchange was seen as beneficial, and the openness of churches to one another made the process of reception easy. One of many possible examples is the widespread reception of the epiclesis in the divine liturgy of the East during the fourth century. Both the influence of controversies over the divinity of the Third Person of the Trinity and, probably, the epiclesis of Hippolytus's *Apostolic Tradition* played a role. There is no doubt that the reception of the epiclesis was a major factor in the development of the Eastern theology of the Eucharist. A number of liturgical feasts spread through the church and were received. Marian feasts such as the Purification, the Nativity, and the Presentation gradually spread from the East into the Western church and especially into the church at Rome. Too, local canonization of saints took place in the West until the thirteenth century. This practice was viewed as a liturgical fact rather than a juridical decision, and by means of reception between churches, a local cult would be extended. Not all such exchanges were positive. Sometimes local practices were lost, and original liturgies could be distorted by subsequent alterations. But at least in the early centuries dangers were recognized and the reception of different liturgical practices was accompanied by an insistence on the freedom of the local church to determine its own liturgical practices. Both Ambrose of Milan (*De sacramentis* 3.1.5) and Gregory the Great (*Epistle* 1.43) show appreciation for local variation.

This attitude was reflected in the early church with regard to laws and customs as well. There were both a toleration of and a will toward reception. Gregory the Great in a response to Augustine of Canterbury shows a pastoral care for both (*Epistle* 11.64). On the other hand there is certainly evidence of a nonreception of various councils' canons dealing with church life. The Trullan Synod in 692 issued some 102 canons. Pope Sergius, who was not a Westerner by birth, refused to accept these canons in the West, apparently because they had little direct relationship to church life there. The Council of Sardica, which met from 343 to 344, confronted the reverse situation. This Western council, which regarded itself as a general council of the church, promulgated a canon stating that problems between churches should be referred to the bishop of Rome, whose decision should be accepted. Not surprisingly, this canon was never received in the Eastern church.[8]

Another clear example from the first Christian centuries is Scripture itself. The canon of Scripture evolved slowly by a process of reception. Not all the books available to the church became part of the canon. Those that were finally accepted passed through very different histories. Some books, like the four Gospels, rather quickly secured universal acceptance. The Book of Revelation found quick acceptance in the East only to be rejected, then later—and only after a painful process—secure a place in the canon. The Pauline corpus had a fairly easy time of it, but the Epistle to the Hebrews had more difficulty, as did the catholic epistles, which were only slowly accepted in Rome. The canon of the New Testament as it is accepted today was first acknowledged in the fourth century—for example, by Athanasius in *Festal Epistle* 39 from the year 367.

Thus, long before systematic thought was given to the concept of reception, reception was practiced. Implicit in the practice were a view of the church as a community of local churches in fellowship with each other with gifts to share; an understanding of the faith as something to be handed down from generation to generation and as something essentially personal; an awareness that reception takes place in eucharistic communities, involves all members of the communities, and is a continuing process; and an appreciation that reception as this spiritual event of transmission and acceptance is fundamental for the life of the church and Christians.

8. See Kilmartin, "Reception in History," 44.

The coming of the Middle Ages in the West created a new context, in which several of these viewpoints ceased to exist. For example, a new ecclesiology appeared in the West that did not see the church as a community of local churches in fellowship but rather saw it as a universal corporation in which clergy and laity gave advice to the pope on important issues. When an agreement was reached on matters of doctrine and discipline by the appropriate representatives, this was regarded as the inspiration of the Spirit and the consensus of the faithful. The responsibility of all was to accept the decision, and no other form of reception was believed to be needed.[9] The result was that reception was viewed as part of constitutional law. A sharp distinction was made between teaching and learning in the church. One part of the church was considered active and the other passive. With the development of such an ecclesiology, reception as practiced in the patristic church became impossible. Adolf Lumpe has shown how in this period the acceptance of papal decretals in the courts and schools of canon law was designated reception. He points out this usage by Pope Honorius III in his bull *Quinta compilatio decretalium,* and by Pope Boniface VIII in his bull *Liber sextus.*[10] In the *Codex iuris canonici* and the attached *Professio catholicae fidei,* the word *recipere* appears often in the sense of "to recognize," "to approve," or "to sanction."[11] Although this vocabulary can be traced back to the fifth century and the writings of Pope Gelasius I, especially to his *De recipiendis et non recipiendis,* it is apparent that much of the original richness of the concept of reception had been lost. As the Western church grew more hierarchical in nature, reception receded more and more into legal categories. This development did not occur in the East, where at least in theory a vital link was always maintained between reception and the active participation of all the faithful. Even in the West authors like Hincmar of Rheims could as late as the ninth century maintain an ecclesiology that recognized the church as a community and saw ecumenical councils as called by the emperor and made up of

9. Ibid. 35–36; and Johannes Muhlsteiger, "Rezeption-Inkulturation-Selbst-bestimmung," *Zeitschrift fur katholische Theologie* 105 (1983): 268.

10. Adolf Lumpe, "Zu 'recipere' als 'gultig annehmen, anerkennen' im Sprachgebrauch des römanischen und kanonischen Rechts," *Annuarium Historiae Conciliorum* 7 (1975): esp. 129–30.

11. Ibid., 130–31.

numerous bishops who played an active role in reception.[12] But the tendencies that led to Pope Honorius III and Pope Boniface VIII had already set in. Pope Damasus and the synod of 368 had maintained that the ecumenicity of a council required papal approval, and this view was repeated by Leo the Great and Gelasius I. Until the sixteenth century the Western church became increasingly papal and reception more and more a matter of canon law.

The fifteenth century supplies unambiguous evidence of nonreception. As is well known, the original text of the Nicene-Constantinopolitan Creed did not contain the word *filioque*, "and the Son," immediately after the phrase "the Holy Spirit who proceeds from the Father." The insertion of the word in the West gradually spread and soon after the year 1000 was adopted at Rome. But it was never accepted in the East, and since the time of Photius, in the ninth century, it has been an issue of disagreement between East and West. The Council of Florence, meeting from 1438 to 1445, endeavored to secure reunion between the Greek church and the church of Rome. Under political pressure and as part of a scheme of reunion, the Greeks accepted the teaching of the *filioque* but not its addition to the Creed. The plan, however, was short-lived. The compromise at the Council of Florence was never accepted in the East. A number of Orthodox synods refused to ratify the union between the Latins and Greeks. Although regarded by the Roman Catholic church as the sixteenth or seventeenth ecumenical council, the Council of Florence was never successful in making this claim in the East and in having its teachings received there. Thus, in a large segment of the church a council with broad representation and papal approval could not even under diverse formulations substantiate its claim to be faithful to the *consensio antiquitatis*.

The sixteenth-century Reformation in the Western church was in part a reaction against the ever-increasing papal domination of the church. Reformation teaching arose in the environment of the late Middle Ages. It was, at the least, a call for a return to the apostolic norm of the gospel, which according to the Reformers had been clearly identified by the writers of the patristic church. In the heated debates of those years, the Reformers appealed to the need for a

12. Hincmar, *Opusculum LV*, Capit c. 20.

general council freed from papal control. Here the Reformers' views were not always the same, but what was intended was a council that would have authority to the extent that its decisions were in accord with the witness of Scripture. Thus there was a standard for the reception of church decisions as well as an understanding of councils as having no absolute infallibility, something the Reformers believed that they saw adequately demonstrated by the endless series of councils in the history of the church. Yet ecclesial reception was not a matter of indifference to the Reformation. In the history of the Reformation churches, reception processes are conspicuous. For example, the confessions of the Lutheran church make a clear case for the reception of the doctrinal decisions of the early church. A couple of illustrations are at hand.

Article 1 of the Augsburg Confession reveals a reception of the Nicene Creed by the Lutheran Reformers. It states in the German, "Erstlich wird einträchtiglich gelehrt und gehalten, lauts des Beschluss Concilii Nicaeni," and in Latin, "Ecclesiae magno consensu apud nos docent, decretum Nicaenae synodi . . . credendum esse."[13] Article 3 of the Confession is an indication of a reception of the Apostles' Creed by the same Reformers.[14] The desire to identify with the creeds of the early church was expressed not only by Lutherans. Parallels to articles 1 and 3 of the Augsburg Confession exist in the Confessio Helvetica Posterior of the Reformed tradition. The Heidelberg Catechism adopted the Apostles' Creed. Both documents show the wish of the Reformers to adopt decisions of the early church. Article 7 of the Augsburg Confession is concerned with the church. In speaking of what is required for true unity, reference is made to agreement about the teaching of the gospel and the administration of the sacraments.[15]

13. The confessions of the Lutheran churches may be found in the original German or Latin in *Die Bekenntnisschriften der evangelisch-lutherischen Kirche* (Göttingen: Vandenhoeck & Ruprecht, 1959). The best Engl. trans. is *The Book of Concord*, trans. and ed. Theodore G. Tappert (Philadelphia: Fortress Press, 1959). Tappert's trans. (p.27) of the German: "We unanimously hold and teach, in accordance with the decree of the Council of Nicaea . . ." Tappert's trans. of the Latin: "Our churches teach with great unanimity that the decree of the Council of Nicaea . . . should be believed without any doubting."

14. *Book of Concord*, 29–30.

15. Ibid., 32. Tappert's trans. of the Latin: " . . . it is enough to agree concerning the teaching of the Gospel and the administration of the sacraments."

Here the Latin is clearer than the German: ". . . satis est consentire de doctrina evangelii et de administratione sacramentorum," as opposed to ". . . dies ist gnug zu wahrer Einigkeit der christlichen Kirchen, dass da einträchtiglich nach reinem Verstand das Evangelium gepredigt und die Sakrament dem gottlichen Wort gemass gereicht werden." Behind both texts, however, stands awareness of the need for consensus in the church which is based on the reception of certain teachings by all the community.

This acceptance by the Reformers of the need both to receive and to interpret earlier doctrinal decisions of the church was in time extended to the Reformation confessions themselves. The confessional documents in turn were received by the churches formed out of the events of the sixteenth century. Their validity was not based upon an approval by a church magisterium. On the contrary, the Reformers insisted that authority of the confessions rested on their claim to be faithful witnesses and interpreters of Scripture. In the course of time these confessions were no longer considered merely the writings of individuals. The churches of the Reformation assumed a responsibility for them. In the case of the Book of Concord, of 1580, the claim was made not only that the Lutheran churches were speaking but that the one holy, catholic, and apostolic church could find its teaching in these confessions. Thus as confessions they make the claim to be the obligatory model of all of the church's preaching and teaching without limit of time or space. The complete title of the Book of Concord illustrates this status of the confessions and the importance of their reception within the churches. It reads, "Concordia: Christian, Reiterated, and Unanimous Confession of the Doctrine and Faith of the undersigned Electors, Princes, and Estates who Embrace the Augsburg Confession and of their Theologians, Together with an Appended Declaration, Firmly Founded on the Word of God as the Only Norm, of Several Articles about which Disputation and Strife Arose after the blessed Death of Martin Luther, Prepared for Publication by the Unanimous Agreement and Order of the aforementioned Electors, Princes, and Estates for the Instruction and Admonition of their Lands, Churches, Schools, and Descendants."[16] The same ideas are to be found at the conclusion of the first part of the Formula of Concord.

16. Ibid., 1.

The signers declared that they were describing not only their own faith but the faith of all pious Christians who stand with the Word of God, the three creeds, and the earlier Lutheran confessions.[17] The ideas of *consensio antiquitatis* and *consensio universitatis* which we saw as playing such a key role in the acceptance of early councils of the church were not matters of indifference to the Reformers. They stated their claim that their teaching, in distinction from Rome's, did have antiquity and universality. As Luther put it, "I hold, together with the universal church, the one universal teaching of Christ, who is our only master."[18]

As in the case of documents we have observed from the early church, reception of the various sixteenth-century Reformation documents was not immediate. The process continued even after the completion of the formulation of confessions in the sixteenth century. While it is true that no further documents were accorded such confessional basis, the number of officially recognized confessions varies in the different churches of the Reformation. Even within Lutheran churches this is true. Many churches give greater weight to the Augsburg Confession and Luther's Small Catechism than to the other documents. In fact the constitution of the Lutheran World Federation mentions only these two. Some Lutheran churches have refused to recognize the Formula of Concord as a confession and have seen it as the beginning of post-Reformation developments.

An excellent review of the process of the reception of the Augsburg Confession has been provided by Wolf-Dieter Hauschild.[19] Showing the various vicissitudes in the history of the document within Lutheranism, he traces the career of this critical Lutheran confession from its conception in 1530 until the twentieth century. The situation is much more complex than is supposed by the view that the Augsburg Confession attained a preeminent position in Lutheran church life and theology by the middle of the sixteenth century and continued to hold

17. Ibid., 500–501.

18. Martin Luther, *Sincere Admonition to All Christians*, in *Luther's Works*, vol. 45, ed. Walther I. Brandt (Philadelphia: Muhlenberg Press, 1962), 70–71.

19. Wolf-Dieter Hauschild, "Das Selbstverstandnis der Confessio Augustana und ihre kirchliche Relevanz im deutschen Protestantismus," in *Evangelium-Sakramente-Amt und die Einheit der Kirche*, ed. Karl Lehmann and Edmund Schlink (Freiburg im Breisgau: Herder & Herder, 1982), 133–63.

it without interruption until the present time. Anyone interested in the reception of Reformation texts in churches of the Reformation should give careful attention to Hauschild's work. It becomes clear that different interpretations of the Confession continually modify the sense in which it claims authority. This is a point that has also been made by Ulrich Kühn in his work on the rereading of the Augsburg Confession as an authoritative form of the Christian tradition.[20] Kühn demonstrates how the Augsburg Confession must be viewed as a subject and object in the church's process of tradition.

Reception in the sixteenth century, as in the patristic church, should not be seen as limited to theological documents. Even the confessions must be seen in the context of a larger reception that was ongoing —that began with the Reformation and continued beyond it. Many aspects of this progress were not formal, but they were still real. Forms of piety and church life, structures of church organization, hymns, devotional writings, and theological ideas—often different in comparison with what immediately preceded them—were in various stages of the process of reception in the Western church because of the explosive force of the Reformation. They would continue to have their influence felt within the Protestant churches and affect the relations of those churches with the Roman Catholic church for centuries.

During this period the Council of Trent was meeting, from 1545 to 1563. The results of this council—a council that embodied the Counter-Reformation—were certainly not received by the Protestants, and for many Catholics were less than they hoped. Yet the council provides us with another example of reception in the sixteenth century. The teachings of Trent were overwhelmingly received by the Roman Catholic church, with its clearly formulated doctrinal systems.

In theory, reception even of new theological statements should always be a possibility for the Protestant churches. Practically, such reception has occurred very seldom if at all since the sixteenth century. The only two possible cases of it are the Barmen Declaration, of 1934, and the Leuenberg Agreement in its final form of 1973. But widely different views are held about the authority of the Barmen Declaration, and the Leuenberg Agreement applies directly only to the European situation. The situation is different with the Roman

20. Ulrich Kühn, "The Future of a Tradition," in *LWF Report* 9 (1980): 61–79.

Catholic church, as can be observed in the events surrounding the First Vatican Council, in the last century. Earlier in this chapter we noted the tendency developing within the Western church toward a monarchical view of the church, where the pope as the pinnacle of a hierarchical structure is divorced from the rest of the church. Such an ecclesiology eliminates any real need for a broad basis of reception actively involving all the bishops and faithful of the church. This tendency reached its ultimate realization in the pontificate of Pius IX and the First Vatican Council, meeting in 1869–70, one of the results of which was the definition of papal primacy and infallibility. The only aspect of this council of interest here is the reception of its results in the Roman Catholic church. Because of political events the council was formally suspended on October 20, 1870. In view of Pius IX's own understanding of the papal office and the decisions made by the council, especially *Pastor aeternus*, defining the infallibility of the Roman pontiff, one might think that there would be little need for—or attention given by the Roman Catholic church to—a reception of the First Vatican Council's conclusions. The definition itself already implies its reception. Yet at the council a minority opposed *Pastor aeternus*. After the council was disbanded, this minority continued for a while to argue against the council's decision but gradually accepted it. In the course of time they sought as individuals to explain why they had not approved the definition at the council but were later able to do so. It would be interesting to know whether these bishops finally agreed with the definition because they saw it as binding on all or whether in their assent they saw the last necessary capstone of the definition. This is not easy to decide, but the first possibility seems the more likely.[21] Thus one sees a reception by the minority through a process after the council. Johannes Beumer refers to the pastoral letter of August 18, 1870, sent by the German bishops to their dioceses urging support of the council's decisions.[22] Other efforts to secure popular reception of the council's conclusions are documented.[23] These efforts show that in the years immediately after the close of the First Vatican Council a worldwide reception of its decisions occurred in the Roman Catholic

21. Johannes Beumer, S. J., "Das Erste Vatikanum und seine Rezeption," *Münchner Theologische Zeitschrift* 27 (1976): 261.
22. Ibid., 264–65.
23. Ibid., 265–68.

church. This can be seen too in the Roman Catholic church's cat-
echisms and religious manuals. What all this reveals is that even in the
post–First Vatican Roman Catholic church, with its high view of the
papacy, earlier understandings of reception were not totally lost. A
valid council does not depend just on the pope or even just on the
pope with the collegium of bishops. Somehow the larger church is involved. Theologians would debate whether a broader reception only
brings to explicit validation what is already present in a council's
definition or whether the validation of a decree requires the addition
of the general binding power. The argument would tend to the conclusion that a broad reception cannot alter the inner being of a conciliar
decree and that nonreception by the total church cannot in itself be
taken as a sign of false teaching but may merely mean that the proposed
decree is inopportune.[24] But never was the idea seriously expressed
that the broad reception can be eliminated from the life of the church.
Practically, of course, since 1870 it may have been. Yet it has lived on
as an idea with a long history that was again brought to discussion
and acknowledged by the Second Vatican Council, as we have seen in
chapter 1. *Lumen gentium* 12 describes a process of reception in which
all the faithful of the people of God exercise specific charisms for the
renewal and building-up of the church. It speaks with appreciation of
the sense of faith held by all the faithful.

Because the history of the Eastern churches has been different from
the story in the West that has been described here, some mention
should be made of the understanding of reception in the Orthodox
church. Since councils and synods play an important role in the faith
and life of the Orthodox churches, we can be sure that reception is a
significant concept for Orthodox thought. But for these churches,
reception has an importance that exceeds councils and synods, even if
Orthodox theology has no unified explanation of the nature and role
of reception in the life of the church. Certain themes in Orthodox
reflection about reception can, however, be identified. In contrast to
the West, where reception was very often viewed as limited to
statements of the magisterium made in legal categories, for Orthodox
theologians reception must be seen in the light of a total ecclesiology.
Reception involves agreement with the faith of the church as the final

24. Ibid., 270–72.

authority in matters of belief. It is the fruit of the charismatic work of the Spirit, and as such cannot be brought in a legal fashion under official control. The preserver and defender of the faith is the church itself, the faithful, under the guidance of the Spirit. Thus the Eastern churches have always viewed reception in a less juridical and formal manner, at least as compared with the Western church in some periods. The Orthodox churches see in reception a dialectic between the laity and the clergy, both of whom have a critical role under the inspiration of the Holy Spirit.

These views created a tension in Orthodox thought between, on the one hand, the position that an ecumenical synod is the highest authority and, on the other, the position that its decisions can only become valid when they are accepted by the whole church. In this century, Nikolaj Afanassiev, building on the work of Aleksej Chomjakov, taught that decisions of councils are dependent on the reception by the faithful. But not all Orthodox theologians would accept this conclusion,[25] and intra-Orthodox debate continues on the subject. Yet there *is* agreement that reception is, in the final analysis, spontaneous. It is not organized by juridical forms or directives. It is by no means a general plebiscite, but rather reception has its origin in the action of the Holy Spirit, who dwells in the church, supports it, and maintains it in the true faith. For Orthodox theologians the church is complete only as the body of the faithful. Only in this totality, with the support of the Spirit, is the church capable of infallibility. An ecumenical council is only a delegation from the body of the faithful, and only to the extent that it is faithful to the church as a totality can it make the claim to be ecumenical. According to Orthodox thinking, a council is an organ whose infallibility results from, and is an expression of, the infallibility of the church.[26] For the Orthodox, reception of conciliar decisions, books of Scripture, and similar elements of the faith is possible only to the degree that what is received is seen as a truthful expression of the Tradition, of the gospel. Reception under the Holy

25. Waclaw Hryniewicz, "Die ekklesiale Rezeption in der Sicht der orthodoxen Theologie," *Theologie und Glaube* 65 (1975): 260–63.

26. These ideas are developed further by Liviu Stan in "Concerning the Church's Acceptance of the Decisions of Ecumenical Synods," in *Councils and the Ecumenical Movement,* World Council of Churches Studies 5 (Geneva: World Council of Churches, 1968), 68–75.

Spirit's inspiration has a prophetic character; it is a recognition of the gospel itself. It is a proclamation of the episcopal leadership of the truth in the context of the active support of the faithful of the church. These characteristics reflect an understanding of reception that can be traced far back in Christian history, as we have seen, and that can make a contribution to the understanding and practice of reception in an ecumenical age.

From this rapid survey of reception before the rise of the modern ecumenical movement, several insights can be gleaned. Classical reception was never merely the acceptance of theological texts from church councils. It was never a merely juridical process. Rather, reception has always functioned as a continuing, ongoing process that in a sense has predated the institution of the church. It includes the receipt of God's love in his Son as well as the acceptance of a history and a tradition. Also involved is the constant practice of interpretation and reinterpretation. Reception is not repristination, but it is the lively process of the church's drawing from the resources of its past to seize and accept the present activities of its loving Lord. It always involves one church's willingness to receive from other churches. Thus, it must be maintained that the present moment in the ecumenical movement provides unique and special opportunities and challenges to the churches, many without parallel. Nevertheless, to expect the churches of the present to be actively engaged in reception is to expect them to be involved in a process that is at the heart of their very existence.

Our final chapter will speak not so much about the past and present of reception, the word and the concept, as about reception's future and how the word and concept can be a resource at the next stage of that pilgrimage known as the ecumenical movement.

3

THE FUTURE OF
ECUMENICAL RECEPTION

In our survey of classical reception, we have noted how after the divisions of the Eastern and Western churches, and after the Reformation in the West, differing understandings of reception came to be articulated. Generally for the Orthodox, a council was dogmatically binding when it had been received by the whole church. This could be validated by some future council. In the West, reception was connected with conciliar decisions and the acceptance of canon law. Roman Catholic thought, even after the decisions of the First Vatican Council, did not preclude a process of reception, although with the ecclesiology of this council, reception was often seen as passive acceptance. Roman Catholic theology does teach that a council receives and interprets the decisions of earlier councils. In the confessions and liturgical books of the churches of the Reformation as well, the dogmatic decisions of the early church were received. The binding force of the confessions in these Reformation churches rests upon the process of reception. Their confessional documents are not viewed as the opinions of individual theologians or parties within the churches but, rather, have been received under the gospel, in the sense that one holy, catholic, and apostolic church can find its teaching in them.

We have seen, at the same time, that reception in this classical sense is more than mere acceptance of texts. It goes to the core of the church's being. Reception is a rhythm within the church of receiving and re-receiving from its Lord. This often entails reinterpretation and the application of that which has been received, the gospel, in new situations. When the church loses this rhythm within it, it fossilizes or stagnates. Reception in this broad meaning is an ongoing dimension of the Christian faith even if the term "reception" is not always used.

In Chapter 1 we observed how both the word and concept of recep-

55

tion have moved back to the center of theological discussion. The forces that resulted in that development were largely present in the modern ecumenical movement. The outcome is that although reception, an old subject, is now a matter of attention, it is focused in a new context, the ecumenical movement. This new environment has altered the idea of reception. In this moment of the ecumenical movement, reception is thought of as having features sufficiently different from those it was conceived to have in the past that we distinguish "classical reception" and "ecumenical reception."[1] We shall now explore the future of ecumenical reception, by which we mean all phases and aspects of the ongoing process by which a church, under the guidance of God's Spirit, makes the results of a bilateral or multilateral conversation a part of its faith and life because those results are seen to be in conformity with the teaching of Christ and of the apostolic community, that is, the gospel as witnessed to in Scripture. Because ecumenical reception is a reality of which we have but an initial and partial experience, projecting into the future is not without risk. Yet surely the discussion that has already taken place in ecumenical theology and the insights that we have gained from the historical review of classical reception provide a basis for some reflection on the future of ecumenical reception.

Jean M. R. Tillard, the Dominican scholar, has offered some sound counsel for discussing reception today. He points out that reviving the word "reception" after so much neglect carries a certain danger.[2] If used without adequate concern for definition, the word may become an umbrella term, or a catchall. If "reception" means everything, it will finally mean nothing. There is already evidence that reception is viewed as reconciliation of a superficial sort. The potential that the reception process holds for the ecumenical future will be lost if reception is understood as simply the reestablishment of cordial relations. Tillard rightly stresses too that reception must not be viewed as the total absorption of the weak by the strong. Capitulation is not the same as reception.

As our tentative definition brings out, the basis of reception must be nothing less than the gospel itself, the gospel of the life and teachings

1. See pp. 29–30 above.

2. J. M. R. Tillard, O. P., "'Reception': A Time to Beware of False Steps," *Ecumenical Trends* 14/10 (November 1985): 145–48.

of Christ, held in the apostolic community, witnessed to in Scripture. It must always be insisted that the highest standard for reception of ecumenical results is the witness of Scripture. The question of truth cannot be ignored in favor of purely pragmatic or compromise solutions. Reception will involve a grappling with the gospel itself and with how the gospel is interpreted and proclaimed in new situations. To take the criterion of reception to be Scripture is an appeal neither to proof-texting nor to a return to the past, but it is a reminder that reception is entirely dependent upon a lively new encounter with the gospel. It includes a fresh study, reevaluation, and reconfessing of the gospel as the only standard for communion in the faith. Thus the very basis of reception sets us an extremely difficult task. At the same time it discloses the seriousness of the issues involved. Reception will call the churches to a collective conversion to the claims of the gospel itself. As Tillard puts it, "It is not simply a question of mental understanding *per se*; rather it is a question of mutual understanding based on the apostolic faith."[3] As churches struggle with this foundation of reception, they will understandably employ other standards that they have employed in their life. For some churches, such as the Lutheran and Reformed, these will include the confessions from the Reformation; for the Orthodox churches it will be the Tradition of the early church; for the Roman Catholic church it will be the binding dogmas of its history. As all churches endeavor to grasp the basis of reception, they will be influenced by their structures of church life and their liturgical forms. The challenge will be to be faithful to the witness of Scripture as interpreted by these other standards without letting the extrascriptural standards thwart ecumenical progress. Ecumenical agreements and convergences will force the churches under the gospel to reexamine their denominational criteria. In this process there must be an openness to modifying positions previously held and also to conforming to them, to correlating both continuity and change. Without such candor, a genuine process of reception capable of leading the churches beyond the present ecumenical status quo will never be possible.

In what we have said, it has become obvious that the churches are the agents of reception. Individual theologians and other church

3. Ibid., 146.

leaders will certainly make comments that will influence the churches as they engage in reception, but the final word about the reception of any ecumenically claimed agreement or convergence must be the churches' own. This adds to the complexity of the issue, for the churches today are in a divided state, in what has been described as a preconciliar situation. This means that there is not the agreement in faith between these churches that allows them to come together in an ecumenical council in the same manner that was possible in the early church. Thus the World Council of Churches is not in this sense a council but an organization of churches in a stage prior to a genuine council. The separated churches have different structures and ways of ordering their lives. Not all structures serve equally well for reception. Churches that are strongly congregational in organization will have more difficulty with reception than churches that have a highly centralized structure. Nor can one expect reception to move at the same speed in all churches. But whatever the structure of individual churches, reception will confront all the churches with new problems. The churches will have to examine, accept, make differentiations in, and even decline texts arrived at jointly by their officially appointed representatives and those of the other churches, since the ecumenical agreements or convergences come in a certain sense from the outside to them. Reception in large measure will be a question of whether or not the churches are willing to own the work done by their representatives and by the persons from the other churches. In a final stage of this process, official action by the churches at their highest levels of authority will be required.

Yet such action cannot take place in isolation. Before official, institutional reception by church leadership occurs, a much more extensive process must take place. This process will be less formal and not restricted to decisions about texts. It will be gradual, at times almost imperceptible, and will help prepare the ground for more formal acts of reception. Part of this preliminary stage will involve new experiences and the discovery of new insights among the members of churches. Old attitudes will change. Individual traditions will be seen by church members as part of a larger ecumenical context. Polemics of the past will be put aside. Ecumenical influences will be traced in educational programs and liturgical texts. These things will happen as the results of ecumenical progress are communicated and interpreted within the churches. Without an active sharing of information, this initial phase of the reception process will not occur and the subsequent stage of formal reception will be meaningless. Irrespective of the organs of authoritative teaching in any church, this preliminary stage must actively include the entire people of God in the churches. Unless the faithful are willing under the guidance of the Holy Spirit to recognize and accept the gifts of the ecumenical movement—new insights, new witnesses of truth, and new forms of expression of the apostolic faith—formal reception will not be accomplished. Cardinal Willebrands, president of the Vatican's Secretariat for Promoting Christian Unity, has noted that "in its full form reception embraces the official doctrine, its proclamation, the liturgy, the spiritual and ethical life of the faithful as well as theology as systematic reflection about this complex reality."[4] This extensive view of reception is not only accurate, its appreciation in the churches will be necessary for ecumenical advance. The churches are indeed the agents of reception, but when this is stated a church must be understood in the widest sense, that is, as the baptized people of God. The church in that sense will move from the preliminary stage of reception to an official act that institutionally ratifies reception. If at this stage action is limited to the church leadership, be it a council of bishops, a convention, or a presbytery, it should not be overlooked that the institutional action is rooted in a broad base of support. This official act should not be seen as the end product of reception, for it is simply a step along the way. The danger even at this point is that reception may be viewed as merely an affirmation or welcoming of a text. Even at the stage of an official act, reception is more than a formal, verbal, and noetic exercise. It includes the renewal, fellowship, and unity of the churches. Official reception should open the possibility of further steps and have its influence in other situations or later generations.

When reception is viewed as it is described here—as a process based on the gospel and including all the people of God—some of the artificial limits can be removed. All too often reception is seen as an exercise of academic theologians from predominantly First World churches. Even if to a certain degree understandable, that view distorts the

4. Johannes Cardinal Willebrands, *Address to the Convention of the Lutheran Church in America* (New York: Lutheran Church in America, 1984), 10.

genuine meaning of reception and robs it of some of its potential. Professionally trained theologians certainly have a contribution to make to ecumenical reception, and we should be grateful for the great work they have accomplished, but we must also recognize that they do not have a monopoly in this area. All stages of reception involve the whole baptized people of God with their sense of the faith (*sensus fidelium*, the "sense of the faithful believers"). This includes the theologians and other leadership within the churches but is not limited to them. Only when all elements act in harmony is reception possible.

The challenge of this situation should not be missed. Harmony of the required kind has been rare in the history of the church. All churches—the Orthodox, Protestant, and Roman Catholic churches—have insisted upon the role of the faithful in decisions of faith. Yet in practice either the hierarchy of the churches or the theological faculties have played an excessive if not monopolizing role. The Roman Catholic church, especially since the First Vatican Council, has been seen as a hierarchical organization with the teaching authority belonging to the higher clergy, the bishops in communion with the pope. The Roman Catholic faithful have been expected to give their assent, often passively, to what is presented to them as the Christian faith. Ecumenical reception will force all churches to rethink the active role of the people of God. Orthodoxy and Protestantism will have to return to the sources of their traditions and in their light ensure the more active involvement of all the faithful. The Second Vatican Council—in particular its constitution, *Lumen gentium*—shows an attempt to reverse the relationship between the people of God and the hierarchy in the Roman Catholic church. It can have a long-term influence on this church, and it can be hoped that it will lead to a recognition of the authority of the laity in doctrinal matters even if this has not yet happened.

The active involvement of Christian believers in reception will require reconceptualization. The traditional view of divine revelation as the disclosure of truths and teachings will need to be replaced with an insight into revelation as the self-communication of God. There will need to be the recognition that this revelation is transmitted through the church in ways other than teachings and pronouncements. One-sided preoccupation with theoretical truths will need to be replaced with the sense of faith as a free charisma belonging to all the members of the church. This is at best only beginning to occur. As believers articulate their faith as recipients of God's revelation, we should expect their teaching will be presented in new forms and with new methods. The teaching will be linked directly with a concrete view of Christ's life and with concrete problems, needs, and longings. For example, the study of the Commission on Faith and Order of the World Council of Churches entitled "Towards the Common Expression of the Apostolic Faith Today" shows that the matter is no longer as simple as the recitation of the Nicene-Constantinopolitan Creed of 381.[5] Although this creed will continue to hold a special place, the study early acknowledged that it is important to find new ways of confessing the Christian faith. This acknowledgment is closely related to the need for a more active involvement of all believers in the reception of ecumenical results.

Obviously, believers exist outside First World churches. Ecumenical reception as an ongoing process of the churches must not become the exclusive property of European and North American churches. It is true that up to now the dialogues have largely been products of these churches. The First World orientation is less true of the work of the Commission on Faith and Order of the World Council of Churches. Both the text of *Baptism, Eucharist and Ministry* and the early study materials of "Towards the Common Expression of the Apostolic Faith Today" show that reception by Third World churches is already a factor.[6] The Roman Catholic church and its Second Vatican Council provide an example of recent reception in the Third World.

The Roman Catholic General Conference of Latin American Bishops met in Medellín in 1968 with Pope Paul VI present, and it is an instance of the impact of the Second Vatican Council on Latin America. Medellín reflected strength, weakness, and immaturity all at the same time. Nevertheless its sixteen documents closely followed the method of *Gaudium et spes*. The conference cast each of its documents into a framework of inquiry according to which the document dealt first with the facts and reality, then with the contribution of doctrine,

5. See *Apostolic Faith Today*, ed. Hans-Georg Link, Faith and Order paper 124 (Geneva: World Council of Churches, 1985), esp. 12.

6. See the official responses to *Baptism, Eucharist and Ministry*—e.g., *Churches Respond to BEM*, vols. 1–3, ed. Max Thurian, Faith and Order papers 129, 132, and 135 (Geneva: World Council of Churches, 1986–87); and *Apostolic Faith Today*, ed. Link.

and finally with pastoral recommendations. The conference has been seen as a breakthrough. The Catholic church of Latin America, traditionally a passive recipient of movements and inputs from abroad, entered a new age in which it actively took initiative in light of the council. Medellín is a clear case of the beginnings of reception in a Third World context, although admittedly with but one church. The documents "Justice" and "Peace" were strong in their call for liberation through nonviolent means. But "Justice" and "Peace" were often not related to the documents speaking of "evangelization" and "church structure." What is more, the content of the documents was in advance of the views of some bishops, priests, and laity. If Medellín provided an example of the beginnings of the reception of the achievements of the Second Vatican Council in Latin America, it also created the need for its own process of reception that did not really come to fruition until the Third General Conference of Latin American Bishops, at Puebla in 1979.[7]

The conference at Puebla, attended by Pope John Paul II, built upon Vatican II, Medellín, and Pope Paul VI's *Evangelii nuntiandi.* It aided the churches in Latin America to gain self-identity and to enter into dialogue, communion, and participation within their cultures. It is also a striking example of the participation of laity—a remarkable fact for churches long characterized by clericalism and a distance created by authority between clergy and laity. This contributed much to the force of the call of Puebla for preferential treatment for the poor not only economically and politically but also in evangelization.[8]

Both of these Roman Catholic conferences furnish clues and indications of what ecumenical reception in the Third World context will include in the future: the active participation of the laity, a recognition of deep social needs and concerns, an understanding and appreciation of cultural settings far different from the European and North American. Although in this process a harmony of laity, church leadership, and theologians will be required in all the churches, the different

7. On the conference in Medellín, see *The Church and Culture since Vatican II,* ed. Joseph Gremillion (Notre Dame, Ind.: Univ. of Notre Dame Press, 1985), esp. 56–68.

8. On the conference at Puebla, see *Church and Culture,* ed. Gremillion, 68–72, 235–90; *Puebla and Beyond: Documentation and Commentary,* ed. John Eagleson and Philip Scharper, trans. John Drury (Maryknoll, N.Y.: Orbis Books, 1979); and James A. Scherer, "A Lutheran Perspective on Mission and Evangelism in the Twentieth Century," *LWF Report* 11–12 (1982): 167–70.

structures of authority and decision making in the churches will have their influence. We should not expect the process to be the same in all churches. The structure of some churches will more readily facilitate the process than that of others. All churches will be challenged by ecumenical reception to rethink how they make decisions. For the Lutheran tradition, the responsibility for the teaching of the church, and thus for reception, belongs to the whole church and in a special way to pastors, theological faculties, synods, and bishops. This collaboration of different gifts and responsibilities should find expression in the process of reception. Parishes, assemblies of pastors, bishops, and faculties and communions all have their role. Yet when the Lutheran Church in America endeavored to involve all these constituencies in a process of response, in an initial phase of reception, it became clear that all were being confronted with new questions and that there was some confusion about what was being asked.[9] Confusion continues as the process develops and church conventions are requested to take the results of all this study and formulate official conclusions to dialogue results. Ecumenical reception will remain incompletely realized until the churches themselves face more directly in the new ecumenical setting their need for a clear conception of authoritative teaching which includes theologians, other church leaders, and the faithful. As the churches do this, they must remind themselves that the ongoing process of reception takes place under the guidance of God's Spirit.

The churches can indeed be open to reception, but they must not conclude that they can orchestrate it. Reception is in the final sense a gift of the Spirit. The entire process of reception has to be viewed and placed under the guidance of God's Spirit. The separated churches will welcome new and fresh expressions of the ecumenical movement and discoveries of their common faith only as the Spirit makes this possible. As the churches struggle to take the results of the ecumenical movement and make them part of their faith and life, the gifts of the Spirit will be needed. The need is rooted at the core of the Christian tradition. Openness to the present-day work of the Spirit in the lives of the divided churches is indispensable for the continuing process of

---

9. See, e.g., "Churches Respond to BEM," in *Churches Respond*, ed. Thurian, 1:28–38; and *A Response to "Justification by Faith"* (New York: Lutheran Church in America, 1986).

reception. That is why reception must be perceived as foremost a spiritual process. The recognition of its spiritual character does not make reception vague or abstract. Rather it protects it from being viewed as only a sociological process or a democratic movement looking for a majority vote.[10] The awareness that reception operates under the Spirit keeps the churches open to a common fidelity to the mind and will of Christ himself. Reception becomes not vaguer but more demanding, for it must reflect not a plebiscite in the churches but a willingness of one church to accept from other churches as churches. Hence, reception must never be limited to formal decisions by competent church leaders to accept the conclusions of an ecumenical dialogue as an adequate expression of the faith of their particular church. Genuine reception will not occur if each church keeps judging ecumenical results by how closely they conform to its own beliefs. It will happen as churches become increasingly aware of the work of the Holy Spirit in the ecumenical movement and in other churches.[11]

Thus reception is a process that is both theological and spiritual, for the decisions taken by a church are finally accepted by its members not only because they are theologically correct but because they are seen as faithful to the New Testament, the gospel. The faithfulness of the decisions lies in their harmony with our responsibility to accept and hand on Christ in the power of the Spirit, who in turn is accepted from the Father. Lukas Vischer has declared that the churches need to develop nothing less than a spirituality of reception. For him this includes a receptivity to reforms and to structures of common authoritative decision making. A claimed ecumenical consensus requires the churches to articulate this consensus in new ways in order to make it their own.[12]

The ecumenical tasks will demand an ecumenical formation. Such a formation is more than ecumenical education and interpretation, as important as those are. It is something that perhaps can best be described as a quality of spirit. It is more than tolerance or the sharing

10. See the comments of John Macquarrie in *Theology, Church, and Ministry* (London: SCM Press, 1986), 190–92.

11. I am indebted to the presentation of these ideas by Emmanuel Sullivan, S.A., in "Reception: Factor and Movement in Ecumenism," *Ecumenical Trends* 15/7 (July–August 1986): 107.

12. See Lukas Vischer, "The Process of 'Reception' in the Ecumenical Movement," *Midstream* 23 (1984): 221–33, esp. 233.

of information. Until 1952 the churches in the ecumenical movement were largely called upon to develop an attitude of trust and tolerance, to form casual acquaintances. This was relatively easy. But ecumenical formation is far more difficult and threatening. Now the churches must acknowledge that something of importance has occurred through the ecumenical movement. What has occurred will have to become part of their faith and life. It is more than polite recognition. It involves a will to accept the conclusions of the ecumenical movement and to take the churches beyond where they are now. It is the excitement of claiming a convergence process that will finally lead under the Spirit to some form of visible unity. The churches in the process of this ecumenical formation will have to develop principles for active ecumenical involvement, recognize the ecclesiality of other churches, and reformulate their theological thinking and understanding. Even ecumenical texts will be read differently, not with a prejudgment according to the principles of one tradition but in a spirit of openness and in accord with the method by which the texts were written. So ecumenical reception will call not only for information but for a formation that affects theological thinking, spiritual understanding, and attitudes toward other churches. For reception is the receiving of churches and people.[13] As such, it will summon churches to do certain things.

Our definition of ecumenical reception clearly indicates that we are concerned here with an ongoing process. Reference to this characteristic of reception has been made numerous times in the preceding pages. But just as the churches as the agents of reception must be viewed in the broadest sense, so must the process of reception be understood broadly and not narrowly. Too often there has been a common perception that reception occurs in the time between the appointment of participants in a dialogue and the first reactions to the dialogue's final report. Such a limiting of reception will only distort the understanding of all the elements of a process that collectively should be known as reception.

The initial phases of this process begin long before any dialogue is conceived. The beginnings of reception are to be found in that period of time when churches break out of their own isolation. When a par-

13. See Sullivan, "Reception," 108.

ticular church acknowledges that it is neither the sole bearer of Christian truth nor the only witness to Christian faith, the first stirrings of ecumenical reception take place. Usually such a period of what could be called coexistence is followed by a time of cooperation. Churches now recognize one another as churches to the extent that they are prepared to undertake certain tasks together. There is real, if limited, partnership. Practical collaboration takes place in the areas of community service and of issues concerning social justice. Occasions present themselves for limited forms of common prayer and study. In all these activities, separated churches begin to recognize one another as churches. This is the prerequisite for any later reception.[14] It normally begins prior to any suggestion of dialogue. Actually the step to enter into dialogue reveals that the process of reception is already underway. Genuine dialogue is based upon the fact that separated churches in varying degrees acknowledge one another as church, recognize the positive contributions of one another to Christianity, and identify specific obstacles to greater unity and understanding. Thus any church's decision to enter into dialogue is a major step of ecumenical commitment. The intensity of the process of reception increases.

No doubt ecumenical dialogues will in the future be modified or new ways of ecumenical advance will be found. Probably dialogue participation will be expanded to include more than professionally educated theologians. Topics besides the historically divisive ones of gospel, Scripture, ministry, and ecclesiology will have to be addressed. Even after such expansion and even given the impressive accomplishments that have already occurred, dialogue will need to be supplemented. New ways for churches to grow together will have to be developed which will permit inclusion of the churches that are not well organized at world, regional, and national levels or that do not possess a strong tradition of, and high regard for, dogmatic theology, doctrinal decisions, and liturgical traditions. As such new ways are found—perhaps through councils of churches—they will affect ecumenical reception.

At the present time there is a tendency to see the final report of ecumenical dialogues as if not the conclusion, at least the penultimate

---

14. See William G. Rusch, *Ecumenism: A Movement toward Church Unity* (Philadelphia: Fortress Press, 1985), 116–17.

stage, of reception. Actually the situation is much more complex. The completion of a dialogue opens a new phase of reception. Dialogues normally point beyond themselves. Now the goal is no longer reaching convergence or consensus but the translation of theological agreements into practice in the living fellowship of the churches that have been represented in the dialogue. In the best of circumstances these phases should have some overlap. A dialogue must not surrender the technical work it must do, but ways must be found for the dialogue's direct participants, perhaps in consultation with educators and interpreters, to aid the participating communions to take hold of and evaluate the results. Without sacrificing the technical detail required for theological advances, official reports can by their content and style discourage or encourage reception. For example, the language of *Baptism, Eucharist and Ministry* encourages reception.[15] The participants of a dialogue cannot judge the dialogue's work for the churches. They must allow the work to stand on its own right once it is submitted to the churches. Yet prior to the dismissal of a dialogue team, there may be ways not yet tapped by which the dialogue members can be a resource for the evaluation now beginning. The ways may include a preparation of study materials, commentaries by individual dialogue members, and the availability of dialogue members to serve as resource persons for educational events. Thus the knowledge and experience of the dialogue's participants might be tapped into more vitally as all arenas of the church become involved: clergy, congregations, church leaders, and theologians.

Already there is emerging evidence that after a major ecumenical document is produced, the next stage in the reception is what is becoming known as a "response." A response is the first official word from a church to an ecumenical document. It is far from reception, but it can be a positive sign and incentive to other steps leading to reception. On the other hand, a response that is negative in tone may delay or prevent reception, either by not agreeing with the claims of the ecumenical document or by requiring more work. It is important to note that an initial refusal of a church to make a positive response

---

15. *Baptism, Eucharist and Ministry* is replete with such terminology. See, e.g., "Baptism," secs. 8, 12, 13, 14; "Eucharist," secs. 1, 2, 21, 30, 32; and "Ministry," secs. 5, 7, 14, 16, 20, 27, 40. It is not only in the preface that *Baptism, Eucharist and Ministry* asks for reception.

does not exclude a later positive response or even reception. The history of the church contains many examples of initial nonreception that is superseded by reception, so nonreception should not be taken as an indicator of invalidity. Some of the outstanding examples of this are Nicaea itself, Chalcedon, and Nicaea II. The absence of a positive response or of ecumenical reception may simply mean that for any of a variety of possible reasons the churches in the broadest sense were not willing to act positively, that the teaching did not evoke any voice of identity and commitment from the churches *at a particular moment*. The ever-increasing responses to *Baptism, Eucharist and Ministry* and to various dialogues must be taken with utmost seriousness as evaluations of key documents in the ongoing process of reception, but they should not be thought to pass final judgment. For the responses themselves are rarely a simple vote of approval or disapproval of an ecumenical text. They show that as the churches make their responses, they offer criticism, acceptance, and modification—all at the same time. Even the most positive responses tend to temper their words of encouragement with caveats. This is not surprising, for in reception churches are in the final analysis accepting not ecumenical texts but one another as churches. They are seeking behind the texts a common conviction that they share the same gospel. No doubt a step beyond responses will be the further refinement of existing texts or the production of new texts to add clarity. For many churches and large parts of the ecumenical movement, this stage is just beginning.

The goal of reception still stands before the separated churches. In very few if any cases has ecumenical reception taken place to bring separated churches into full unity, for this is the ultimate goal of reception. Although the *realization* of this goal remains in the future, there is a growing awareness of what is involved in such reception. Reception is not a passive acceptance of something from outside one's immediate tradition. It is not a popularity contest either, nor is it the acquiescence to juridical decisions or the surrender of identity. Rather, reception is a highly active process, with intellectual, spiritual, and practical dimensions. It calls for change and renewal by the churches. Dialogues and their reports cannot by themselves bring about reception, although they can bring the goal nearer. Ecumenical reception as a gift of God's Spirit will have occurred within and among the churches when a communion exists that is rooted in a confession of the one faith, a mutual recognition of churches, a common sacramental life, and a mutually committed community of spiritual life expressed in witness, service, and conciliar consultation.

So ecumenical reception will never be easy. When churches are concerned with it, they are involved at the core of their being. No church should lightly entertain the idea of reception. Major issues of Christian faith, such as views of church, ministry, and authority, will be drawn into reception's ongoing process. The serious undertaking of reception is being realized as the grappling with questions on which the churches have been divided and which they now see can become a cause for mutual enrichment. This is no easy matter for most churches. Reception is urgently raising the dilemma for the churches of how they can remain true to their own traditions at the same time that they develop an openness to the reception of ecumenical results that are not simply a reflection of their own traditions of faith. How do Anglicans, Lutherans, and Roman Catholics, for example, react to ecumenical statements that at least at first glance are not identical with the traditional teachings of their churches? Reception is aided when individual denominations can begin to recognize that some of these ecumenical teachings are not alien to their traditions but have become forgotten or obscured in the course of history. Here ecumenical progress can be greatly aided by historical studies. It is also helpful to recognize that some ecumenical statements express convictions that have been secondary in the various traditions and can legitimately receive greater stress on the grounds of the traditions' own teachings and history. It is useful for churches to appreciate that ecumenical statements can often help correct one-sidedness or weakness in the individual traditions and that no tradition is incapable of benefiting from this corrective effect. All traditions in the ongoing process must ask whether there is a hiatus between their official doctrine and practice. Obviously not all churches will engage in this strenuous process at the same level of commitment. Reception will be a centuries-long process, as it has always been in the church.

Various so-called nontheological factors also influence ecumenical reception. For example, some churches with the same confessional standards have offered very different responses to *Baptism, Eucharist and Ministry*. Logically it would seem that the same confessional standards should result in similar responses, but this has not always been the case. Other factors that have come into play have included the position of a responding church as minority or majority, as well as its status as a Volkskirche or a state church. Even the identity of the chief ecumenical partners in a local situation can affect the character of reception. Is the predominant church Roman Catholic, Orthodox, or free-church, and what has the history of its external relations been? Such factors are not unimportant and will affect the process of ecumenical reception in many places.[16]

Thus, reception has the potential today, as it has always had, not only of healing old divisions but also of creating new ones. The Council of Chalcedon and the reception of its conclusions by some churches resolved a long-standing christological dispute. It created a unity. But at the same time it caused a disunity that is still unhealed today. Ecumenical reception, influenced by nontheological as well as theological considerations, may create greater unity across traditional lines at the same time that it results in greater tensions and disunities within confessional families. This situation will become clear only as ecumenical reception continues in the churches.

As ecumenical reception continues within and among the churches, at least three of its component tasks can be distinguished. There is first of all *reception in the narrow sense.* What is intended here is an owning by the churches of the results of convergence and consensus claimed by those they have deputed to participate in ecumenical dialogues and in the general ecumenical process. The conclusions of convergence or consensus put forth by competent representatives of the churches, coming to the churches from outside, must become ecclesial convergence and consensus. To the fullest degree consistent with integrity, the churches must own the results of multilateral and bilateral conversations. If a church concludes that a particular ecumenical teaching is indeed a faithful witness to the gospel, it must be willing to make it not only formally but also realistically and practically part of its faith and life, even if the teaching speaks in a strange accent to that church's tradition. Until this is accomplished, reception in the broader sense

---

16. For two useful articles on ecumenical reception, and particularly on this aspect, see Günther Gassmann, "Rezeption im 'ökumenischen Kontext,' " *Ökumenische Rundschau* 26 (1974): 314–27; and idem, "Die Rezeption der Dialoge," ibid. 33 (1984): 357–68.

will be stalled. The conviction of some ecumenical scholars is that the dialogues have already solved the major issues that have kept the churches apart for centuries. The challenge then is not to find solutions but to have those solutions become decisive in the churches. This raises for the churches the question of what degree of pluralism is acceptable to them. Only the churches can answer the question, but on their answer depends the progress of ecumenical reception.

A second task of ecumenical reception can be called *nonreception.* What is intended here is a reconsideration and rejection by the churches of those portions of their faith and life that obscure or distort the gospel as it has been understood and proclaimed through the centuries. Every tradition has its peculiarities. Often, they have arisen in the church's history in moments of polemic, and they are frequently a source of pride and rejoicing. But although at the time of their creation they may have been part of the clear identification of the gospel, they today often obstruct the gospel. Churches should embark upon the process of nonreceiving these hindrances. A good example is the many mutual anathemas proclaimed between churches in their attempts to safeguard the gospel. Strong action was not necessarily wrong in its day, but the present situation has changed and the anathemas no longer speak to real church-dividing issues. In order to promote ecumenical reception, the churches should actually go about removing outworn condemnations from the expressions of their faith and life. That is what the Leuenberg Agreement asked the Lutheran and Reformed churches to do in Germany. Recently Lutherans and Roman Catholics in Germany have also been examining the condemnations addressed to each other during the Reformation.[17]

A third task of ecumenical reception can be called *dereception.* The difference between dereception and nonreception may at times seem artificial, but a distinction exists. It lies in the possibility of differentiating between *beliefs and practices in the individual traditions that obscure or distort the gospel as understood through the centuries* (this is what nonreception aims at removing) and *beliefs and practices that, though the gospel is not at stake, hinder the visible unity of the*

---

17. See sec. B.III of the Leuenberg Agreement, reproduced in *An Invitation to Action: The Lutheran-Reformed Dialogue, Series III,* ed. James E. Andrews and Joseph A. Burgess (Philadelphia: Fortress Press, 1984), 68–70; and in *Lutheran World* 20 (1973): 351–52.

church (this is what dereception aims at removing). In the latter category fall those things that Lutherans have described as adiaphora—as, for example, in article 15 of the Augsburg Confession and S.D. 10 of the Formula of Concord. Although there has been, and indeed continues to be, disagreement about exactly what are and remain adiaphora, every Christian tradition should concur that it is important to identify them. When adiaphora make it more difficult for churches to manifest their visible unity, the adiaphora must become part of a process of dereception by the churches. For instance (other examples could be given), the Roman Catholic participants in the Lutheran–Roman Catholic dialogue in the United States spoke of the changes in papal leadership designed to reflect the collegial aspect of church leadership and a view of the papal office as servant of the gospel and not absolute monarch.[18] As all churches identify adiaphora in their life and dereceive them, ecumenical reception will be enhanced and proceed.

The discussion of these last two categories, nonreception and dereception, should not lead to the conclusion that complete uniformity among churches is necessary for ecumenical reception to advance. Whatever the final models of church unity turn out to be, they will certainly include diversity. The diversity will result in part from the churches' refusal to enter into a complete nonreception and dereception. This situation need not be a hindrance to greater unity if what is kept is recognized as appropriate to the life of a specific church, and if other churches can agree that it is not contrary to the gospel. There exists a certain hierarchy of importance in church teachings. Though there would be considerable discussion about the rankings in such a hierarchy, most churches would agree that the Trinitarian and christological doctrines are central to and foundational for Christianity. Thus agreement in these areas and the reception of the agreement by the churches are more important for the ongoing process of ecumenical reception than are nonreception and dereception in other areas. The life of the early church can provide some useful models in this regard, for there are abundant examples from that period of different churches with divergent theologies and liturgies living in a pro-

18. See *Primacy and the Universal Church: Lutherans and Catholics in Dialogue V*, ed. Paul C. Empie and T. Austin Murphy (Minneapolis: Augsburg Pub. House, 1974), 27–28, 37.

found communion because they did not consider their areas of disagreement to affect their common allegiance to the foundational truths of Christianity.

As the churches engage in the process of ecumenical reception, the rate of progress will be determined at least in part by what it is that the churches are asked to receive from other churches. Beliefs and ways of life that seem most compatible to a receiving church will be accepted with less difficulty than those which are strange or which initially appear hostile. Lutheran and Reformed churches should have little problem in receiving the work of their dialogues on justification by grace through faith. Each tradition should hear what in the other is compatible with and similar to its own position. On the other hand, Lutherans will have more difficulty in receiving certain recommendations of their national and international dialogues with Roman Catholics when these recommendations ask Lutherans to alter some of their earlier judgments about the papacy. Conversely, contemporary reception of some teachings of Martin Luther's that are recommended by the same dialogues will encounter obstacles among Roman Catholics.

Here it appears that there are some parallels between ecumenical reception and inculturation. If inculturation has to do with the expression of the Christian faith in different cultures from those in which the faith was first expressed, ecumenical reception is in some ways similar. Inculturation raises questions of how black Africans or South Americans must take responsibility for Africanizing or South-Americanizing Christianity; ecumenical reception asks, for example, that Lutheran Christians be responsible for receiving some aspects of Anglican or Roman Catholic Christianity and integrating them into their particular tradition, as it does that Anglicans and Roman Catholics integrate some aspects of Lutheran Christianity into theirs. Perhaps the parallels should not be pushed too far, but ecumenical reception may gain if those responsible for it in the churches give some attention to the growing literature about inculturation.[19]

The attempt to find specific examples of ecumenical reception quickly reveals how little has been accomplished and how much is still

---

19. See, e.g., Amy R. Crollius, "What Is New about Inculturation? A Concept and Its Implications," *Gregorianum* 59 (1978): 721–38; Johannes Mühsteiger, "Rezeption-Inkulturation-Selbstbestimmung," *Zeitschrift fur katholische Theologie* 105 (1983): 261–89; and Hans B. Meyer, "Zur Frage der Inkulturation der Liturgie," ibid., 1–31.

before the churches. Ecumenical reception is in its earliest stages. The examples we have must be viewed not only as few in number but as preliminary in development. Still, ecumenical reception has already occurred between churches in a number of important areas. Often this reception has been informal in the sense that one cannot point to official and juridical acts. Nevertheless it is real and has implications for the future. There is today among churches in the ecumenical movement a far-reaching recognition of one another's baptism. In many churches new worship materials reflect the acceptance of liturgical prayers and hymns from many traditions. In the United States the *Lutheran Book of Worship* is merely one example of several that could be cited. Hymn texts of Martin Luther's are being sung by Roman Catholics. The so-called Lima liturgy, although not an official document of the Commission on Faith and Order of the World Council of Churches, is based on *Baptism, Eucharist and Ministry* and has enjoyed widespread use. Here reception is not a matter of dogmatic formulation, but as affirmation at the level of the daily life of the vast majority of Christians it produces a climate nourished by the common practice of faith. In such a climate it is only reasonable to expect that the entire process of ecumenical reception will thrive.

A significant example of ecumenical reception can be seen in the Roman Catholic church in its Second Vatican Council. As Cardinal Willebrands reminded the Lutheran Church in America in 1984, the Roman Catholic church in its Second Vatican Council received the ecumenical movement. The Cardinal pointed out that this reception was not simply a matter of conciliar documents. The Roman Catholic church has made considerable effort to develop principles and methods for active participation in the ecumenical movement, including dialogue with the Orthodox church and the churches springing from the Reformation. He described how entry into the ecumenical movement was prepared for in the preconciliar period in theology, in the Christian life of the faithful, and hesitatingly, in some statements of the Roman Catholic magisterium.[20] Certainly the process of ecumenical reception in the Roman Catholic church is ongoing, as it is in other churches. Critics have observed that the process in the Roman Catholic church has been great although uneven and has be-

---

20. See Willebrands, *Address to the Convention of the Lutheran Church in America*, 9.

queathed both possibilities and uncertainties to the future. But we should not minimize this instance of continuing ecumenical reception. Ecumenical history between 1965 and the present, as well as the ecumenical future, is marked by the Roman Catholic church's reception—in many ways quite unpredictable—of the ecumenical movement.

The Leuenberg Agreement can also be regarded as an instance of ecumenical reception. This document was mentioned in chapter 1 to illustrate how ecumenical conclusions call for reception. Here we may observe how the sponsoring churches accepted the challenge of reception.[21] The Leuenberg Agreement was the result of dialogue between Lutheran and Reformed churches in Europe. Realized in 1971 and submitted to the sponsoring churches, the document was revised at Leuenberg in 1973, and the churches were asked to give their approval by September 30, 1974. The long history behind the agreement reaches back to the Wittenberg Concord, of 1536, and includes such important documents in this century as the consensus on theses produced in Holland in 1956 and the Arnoldshain Theses, produced in Germany in 1959. The participants in the Leuenberg conversations were officially appointed by their churches. The conference in 1973 included forty-five delegates from sixteen countries; most were church leaders, including legal experts. The agreement is not lengthy.[22] It contains a message to the participating churches, a presentation of the procedure and form for reception, the wording of the actual agreement, and comments on the declaration and realization of church fellowship based on a consensus reached in an understanding of the gospel so that churches with different confessional positions accord to each other fellowship in Word and Sacrament. The Leuenberg Agreement shows that ecumenical reception does not require the exchange of voluminous texts. What is accepted by the churches, more than a text itself, is the body of faithful witnessed to in the text. The participants accord to each other fellowship in Word and Sacrament. The agreement does not establish a static relationship but provides for continuing conversations and opportunities for the churches to grow in consensus. Most European Lutheran and Reformed churches have

21. See p. 25 above.
22. See *An Invitation to Action*, ed. Andrews and Burgess, 61–73.

signed the agreement, and in 1986 the United Evangelical Lutheran Church in Argentina became a signatory. A recent study in Germany which describes the reception of the Leuenberg Agreement in four German Lutheran churches[23] shows that the process of reception has involved pastors, parishes, and the church leadership, all of whom have been called upon to help determine whether the agreement reflects the faith of their churches. The considerations opposing the agreement varied in the churches studied, and what is proved above all else is that the road to ecumenical reception is not smooth. In two of the churches, opposition to the agreement centered on the understanding of biblical and confessional teachings. The resistance of the bishop was a major factor in the case of the third church. The process of ecumenical reception inaugurated by the Leuenberg Agreement is continuing. How the formal acceptance of the agreement will affect the churches and their relations must be observed in the coming years. But until now the Leuenberg Agreement is one of the rare instances where a number of churches have officially acted upon the results of a dialogue and are endeavoring to live out the results and their implications. The Leuenberg Agreement will undoubtedly be an important test case and learning experience for ecumenical reception.

Another example of ecumenical reception comes from the United States; it too discloses that ecumenical reception involves acceptance not only of dialogue texts but also of the insights and results of a dialogue process. In 1982 the American Lutheran Church, the Association of Evangelical Lutheran Churches, and the Lutheran Church in America, along with the Episcopal Church in the USA, concluded the Lutheran-Episcopal Agreement.[24] The actual text of the Lutheran-Episcopal Agreement, like that of the Leuenberg Agreement, is not long—only a few pages. The convergences and consensus expressed in it are based upon three dialogues, two Lutheran-Episcopal dialogues in the United States and one international Lutheran-Anglican dialogue. As a result of the dialogue process, the four

23. Hermann Brandt, ed., *Kirchliches Lehren in ökumenischer Verpflichtung: Eine Studie zur Rezeption ökumenischer Dokumente* (Stuttgart: Calwer Verlag, 1986).

24. *The Lutheran-Episcopal Agreement: Commentary and Guidelines* (New York: Division for World Mission and Ecumenism, Lutheran Church in America, 1983). For developments since 1982, see *What Can We Share? A Lutheran-Episcopal Resource and Study Guide,* ed. William A. Norgren (Cincinnati: Forward Movement Pubs., 1985).

churches in the agreement entered into a process of reception of one another as church. Their agreement holds forth the goal of full communion, acknowledges the participating churches as indeed churches in which the gospel is proclaimed, encourages joint prayer and study as well as cooperation in other areas, provides for interim sharing of the Eucharist in specific situations, and calls for further dialogue on points that are still unresolved. The four participating American churches not only approved the agreement in official action in their general conventions but since 1982 have been active in implementing its provisions. They see themselves to be committed to a process leading to full communion. Thus the Lutheran-Episcopal Agreement in the United States is one of the few examples of ecumenical reception where churches have taken seriously the work of several dialogues, studied it, refined it at several points, and then sought to adopt it officially and live by the results. As Lutherans and Episcopalians complete the next stage of their dialogue and endeavor to press farther down the road of ecumenical reception, additional information will become available about the entire process. This will be widely useful, since many churches, with many ecumenical documents, are on the verge of entering new phases of ecumenical reception. There will be much to learn as the churches continue to respond to *Baptism, Eucharist and Ministry* and then by various processes of reception take the insights of that document into their life. The Anglican communion and the Roman Catholic church will soon issue responses to the international dialogue of the Anglican–Roman Catholic International Commission. The responses will be an important indication of the eventual reception of the dialogue's work in both churches. In the United States, Lutheran and Reformed churches are moving from the response stage to the reception stage of their several dialogues. It is quite possible that within the next decade, certainly by the end of the century, the reality of ecumenical reception will no longer be initial nor will it be as partial as it was perceived to be in 1984.[25]

In an image that is quite powerful to me, Professor Harding Meyer, the director of the Institute for Ecumenical Research at Strasbourg, once spoke of the work of ecumenical dialogues as the discovery of a new land. He went on to say that reception is the opening and the set-

---

25. See p. 31 above.

tlement of that new land[26] and that the settlement may take more time, patience, and effort than the discovery. This picture is one with powerful biblical reflections. It can help to remind Christians and their churches today that with reception—an ecumenical opportunity — they may be given an entrance by the Spirit into a new land where their divisions of the past have finally been overcome and where God's people possess the kind of unity for which their Lord prayed.

26. Harding Meyer, "Rezeption—vom Konsens zur Gemeinschaft," in *Das Ringen um die Einheit der Christen*, ed. H. Fries (Düsseldorf: Patmos Verlag, 1983), 172.